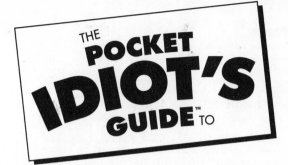

THE **POCKET IDIOT'S GUIDE** TO

# Performance Appraisal Phrases

*by Peter Gray and John H. Carroll*

**ALPHA**

A member of Penguin Group (USA) Inc.

## ALPHA BOOKS

Published by the Penguin Group

Penguin Group (USA) Inc., 375 Hudson Street, New York, New York 10014, U.S.A.

Penguin Group (Canada), 10 Alcorn Avenue, Toronto, Ontario, Canada M4V 3B2 (a division of Pearson Penguin Canada Inc.)

Penguin Books Ltd, 80 Strand, London WC2R 0RL, England

Penguin Ireland, 25 St Stephen's Green, Dublin 2, Ireland (a division of Penguin Books Ltd)

Penguin Group (Australia), 250 Camberwell Road, Camberwell, Victoria 3124, Australia (a division of Pearson Australia Group Pty Ltd)

Penguin Books India Pvt Ltd, 11 Community Centre, Panchsheel Park, New Delhi—110 017, India

Penguin Group (NZ), cnr Airborne and Rosedale Roads, Albany, Auckland 1310, New Zealand (a division of Pearson New Zealand Ltd)

Penguin Books (South Africa) (Pty) Ltd, 24 Sturdee Avenue, Rosebank, Johannesburg 2196, South Africa

Penguin Books Ltd, Registered Offices: 80 Strand, London WC2R 0RL, England

**Note:** This publication contains the opinions and ideas of its authors. It is intended to provide helpful and informative material on the subject matter covered. It is sold with the understanding that the authors and publisher are not engaged in rendering professional services in the book. If the reader requires personal assistance or advice, a competent professional should be consulted.

The authors and publisher specifically disclaim any responsibility for any liability, loss, or risk, personal or otherwise, which is incurred as a consequence, directly or indirectly, of the use and application of any of the contents of this book.

Most Alpha books are available at special quantity discounts for bulk purchases for sales promotions, premiums, fund-raising, or educational use. Special books, or book excerpts, can also be created to fit specific needs.

For details, write: Special Markets, Alpha Books, 375 Hudson Street, New York, NY 10014.

*Dedicated to the managers and supervisors in the work world who want to do employee appraisals right but don't always have the right words to be right.*

# Contents

# Introduction

If you're a new manager—or a small business owner or entrepreneur who's never managed before—you're probably nervous about the first performance appraisal you have to give. Or maybe you're a seasoned executive who's noticed, perhaps much to your chagrin, how much the face of business and management has changed over the past several years. Performance appraisals are an integral part of your responsibilities. More is required today on behalf of your company's human resources' policies, and today's savvy employees expect more from you. The end result is more work, and time, on your behalf, when preparing, writing, and delivering performance appraisals.

Maybe you're worried you'll say the wrong thing or not say the right thing—either way, not be true to your direct reports. Or maybe you've done many reviews in the past but now HR has given you a new, thick set of guidelines to follow to avoid any potential lawsuits from "disgruntled" employees.

Whatever your situation, you're in luck. With the help of this book, you'll see that giving perform-ance appraisals is only as difficult as you make it. The process is straightforward—but full of pitfalls if you're not prepared. And that's our goal: to get you up to speed on giving performance appraisals and to avoid major headaches going forward.

We take you through topics such as preparation, planning, and communicating the appraisal. We have chapters devoted to performance phrases dealing with all types of functions and job activities, including the tough soft personal traits of your employees. We also address special situations and circumstances.

Whether you're a new manager or even a seasoned executive who wants to comply with new or updated human resources guidelines, this book is designed to help you give your employees fair, accurate, honest, and meaningful appraisals.

## How to Use This Book

This book is divided into three parts:

**Part 1, "Performance Appraisals 101,"** outlines the challenges and issues you face as a manager tasked with giving performance appraisals, and covers techniques you can use to overcome them.

**Part 2, "What to Say: Phrases,"** is likely the section (along with Part 3) you'll use most often. Here we give you sample phrases to use on your employees' performance appraisals organized alphabetically by attribute.

You know how it is: you're writing a performance appraisal and you just can't think of the right word. **Part 3, "What to Say: Words,"** gives you some useful key words to describe performance.

As you read through these parts, and especially the phrases and words, you might think some seem judgmental. They must be. To accurately assess, you must make judgments. Just be sure to back up

each judgment with several tangible examples—or
better yet, solid documentation.

## Signs You'll See Along the Way

To supplement the text and what you're learning
about giving performance appraisals, we've in-
cluded some extra info in sidebars. Here's what
you'll see in the chapters:

> ### Performance Pointers _____
>
> These helpful tips and facts give you more
> understanding of the subject at hand.

> ### Performance Pitfalls _____
>
> If you fail to heed these warnings, there
> could be big trouble in your future!

## Acknowledgments

Both authors have a number of people to thank
for helping this book come to fruition. Both of us
are so grateful for the love and support of our
incredible wives, Alisa and Carla. Without their
understanding (and patience with our crazy writing
habits), we could never have completed this. Our
parents and families have been wonderful beyond
words. And our friends have never tired throughout

our hours of talking their ears off about this subject. We especially thank our agent, Marilyn Allen, of the Allen O'Shea Literary Agency. We couldn't have done it without her.

We certainly hope you enjoy this book as much as we enjoyed writing it.

## Trademarks

# Performance Appraisals 101

The performance appraisal is a process feared by subordinates and managers alike. Although many managers routinely give performance appraisals, they sometimes wing it and hope for the best. They fear that their appraisal will not meet with human resources' expectations, and this is often the case. However, with proper resources, organization, planning, and documentation, it will almost always go smoothly.

# Chapter 1

# The Manager's Challenge

## In This Chapter

- Understanding a manager's role
- Knowing what to measure and how to measure it
- Drawing conclusions
- Reviewing key elements of an appraisal

As a supervisor, manager, or executive of a company, organization, nonprofit, volunteer group, or other entity, you have two spheres of operation. You manage production, budgets, programs, processes, services, schedules, and so on. You also lead people; you motivate, challenge, coach, counsel, set goals, provide feedback, develop talent, and build teams. One of your responsibilities is to assess employee performance and provide feedback—otherwise known as the performance appraisal process.

# Setting the Standard: Your Role as Manager

As a manager, you are responsible for setting your employees' performance standards and often the methods by which you measure their performance. You're charged with communicating, in an objective manner, each employee's actual performance against these standards. Is the employee meeting your expectations? Is he or she fulfilling the duties of the position as outlined in the job description? Are his or her business and personal goals being achieved?

Sounds simple enough: set standards and goals, monitor and measure, and provide feedback and corrective action to the employee if necessary. In reality, however, assessing employee performance and writing appraisals is one of the most difficult and perhaps dreaded tasks for managers. It involves people who are not perfect. It requires good writing and communication skills, which most of us have but likely are not as confident in as we'd like to be. It sometimes involves conflict or disagreement because the personalities of your employees are wide and varied. What looks to be simple turns out to be complex.

The task is complicated by the fact that you were likely promoted to your current position of responsibility because you were a great employee. You got the job done, you achieved your goals, and you were knowledgeable in your function.

Yet the skill sets needed to be an effective manager and leader are drastically different from those for being an engineer, accountant, production worker, salesperson, or whatever your job was before you were promoted to a management position. Perhaps this is why you shy away from doing the necessary (and important) work of appraising performance. It is new to you; it involves people. That might be an area you're not comfortable with or confident in just yet.

If you look back at the days before your promotion to management, when you were working solo, you might remember that you sought guidance from your own boss. You wanted to know what was expected of you, what your duties were, and the standards by which you would be measured. You wanted to know what your goals were for the upcoming period.

Your employees will likely have the same questions and expectations of you that you had of your manager. By laying out your expectations for them, you will help them maximize their chances for success.

## Measuring Greatness

Employees essentially want to perform, to achieve, to grow, and to advance in responsibility and pay. They also want feedback. There are many ways to provide this feedback, but the annual performance appraisal is the main vehicle for recording and communicating this information. It is a formal process with many implications for both employee and manager:

- Salary increases are often based on individual ratings.

- Where bonuses are paid, they may be based on overall performance and whether the employee met specific objectives.

- Performance results are used to identify high-potential employees the company might be able to target for special development and training.

- Promotions are typically awarded to employees whose performance levels have been rated exceptional.

And just as good ratings beget rewards and recognition, adverse performance ratings signal an employee's job might be in jeopardy. Performance ratings drive employee rankings, which are used during downsizings and layoffs.

### Performance Pitfalls

Be sure you're being honest in your appraisals. Many new managers want to be buddy-buddy with their team, and this only leads to disaster. We guarantee it. Being friends with your subordinates makes you ineffective as a manager, which is to the detriment of all concerned.

Because of all that's riding on them, many managers approach writing and communicating employee performance appraisals with apprehension—the same goes for the employees receiving them. The goal of this book is to strengthen your appraisal skills; to give you the basics of creating successful appraisals; and provide you with the essentials to give clear, exact reviews to your employees.

# Gathering Data

In almost any company, you, the manager, are tasked with gathering data about your employees' performance during a past period, usually the past 12 months. Armed with that information, you can set up an objective assessment of the overall employee performance, including ratings for individual duties and past goals. The appraisal most likely contains *quantitative ratings* but also *qualitative ones*.

Frequently, quantitative issues are easily identified and measured because numerous *metrics*—department or individual financial performance, sales results, margins, productivity or efficiencies, production output, level of quality, etc.—around one's job are readily available or easily established. In the end, either the person did or did not accomplish the set goal or duty.

The later assessment, the qualitative, deals with less-tangible and less-measurable performance standards. For example, production rates or efficiencies are easily measured. But how do you measure things such as communication or interpersonal skills, ethics, attitude, reliability, problem-solving, or being a team player? What are appropriate traits, and how do you summarize your assessment in words? This is where you draw from your vocabulary, writing skills, and use of appropriate phrases. If you're a manager who agonizes over your choice of words, you're in luck, because Parts 2 and 3 of this book provide a detailed lexicon of performance appraisal phrases for a variety of jobs, tasks, personality traits, and behaviors.

The task of gathering performance data is easier if you set clear expectations at the beginning of the performance period. What are the duties of the job? Job standards? Metrics? Functional and personal goals? With clearly defined parameters, you can more easily check to see how an employee is doing throughout the year and at the end of the performance period—actual versus expected or planned, real versus budget, etc.

In some instances, such as production employees, output and quality are readily available statistics. Some circumstances exist where testing is an acceptable method of measuring knowledge, although it doesn't always mean that the individual does the work satisfactorily. On-the-job observations provide essential awareness that the person does or doesn't do the task in an acceptable manner.

You also should seek the input of the employee and those who work around him or her. Many appraisal programs call on the employee to complete a similar or identical form to the one the manager completes, with a self-assessment on the same tasks, terms, goals, and so on. Many companies have in place a 360-degree feedback process. These are surveys, often electronic, of a sample of the employee's co-workers, customers, subordinates, and so forth, so a full sphere circle of sources is tapped for information on evaluating the employee.

 **Performance Pointers**

Consider keeping an incident file on each of your employees. When you observe a situation of unique or poor performance, immediately relay this to the employee, compliment or correct him, and also drop a note to his file with the date, a description of the incident, and the action taken. You can also keep e-mails, letters, transcripts of voicemails from people who interact with your employee, and so forth.

## Translating Data

After you have gathered all the appropriate data, you're ready to draw your conclusions about the employee's performance and the achievement of (or failure to achieve) his goals, including specific ratings and verbiage for each job element. Again, you may be required to follow company-approved forms to rate and record your performance assessment decisions. In other instances, you may have a blank piece of paper on which to list responsibilities, tasks, goals, behaviors, etc. that were agreed to at the beginning of the performance period. Along with these, you write your conclusions of how the employee has met those tasks and goals.

# Appraisal Essentials

Regardless of what format you use to record your assessment, some key elements must be addressed, including the following:

- What is the employee's performance on specific activities and goals? What is the overall performance?

- What is the performance trend? Compared to the prior appraisal period, is the employee's performance improving, staying the same, or declining?

- What are your employee's strengths, and how can they be better utilized in the future?

- What are his or her weaknesses or developmental areas? How has this individual impaired his or her overall performance, and what needs to be done in the future?

- What are your expectations and goals for the next performance period? (These include functional job requirements, improving soft skills, and personal training and development objectives.)

- What will you, as the manager, do to enable your employee to succeed and grow?

**Performance Pointers**

*Soft skills* are intangible skills that are harder to measure and define. Such skills rarely are in the job description, but they are still crucial elements for success, seen in day-to-day operations. A few examples include interpersonal skills, ethics, judgment, leadership, and potential for advancement, among others.

Document all these things on the appraisal form, and be sure to relay each to the employee during your performance appraisal meeting.

## The Least You Need to Know

- Managers must set objectives standards.
- Employees want to achieve. Help them do this by letting them know what your objectives are for them.
- During the assessment, look at easily quantifiable issues as well as qualitative issues.
- Observe employees on the job to view their real-world competence.

Chapter 2

# Planning the Review Meeting

## In This Chapter

- Getting ready: gathering all the proper documents
- Reviewing your objectives
- Deciding what you'll say
- Choosing a meeting time and location

The key to a successful appraisal review meeting is in the planning. Many performance review discussions go awry because the manager is not prepared—and the same goes for the employee. Some managers barely complete the appraisal forms and written comments in time for the employee meeting, not putting in the required planning ahead of time. The meeting with the employee then becomes disorganized, confusing, and perhaps even confrontational, and intent and control of the meeting are both lost. Careful thought about the meeting and your employee's data beforehand are key to a successful meeting.

It's important to complete the appropriate forms and written commentary well before the meeting with your employee. Take notice of internal company deadlines, if applicable, and save yourself the aggravation and pressure of trying to do everything at the last moment, particularly if you have a number of employees to review and meet. This will allow you to prepare for each meeting and document everything you want to discuss with your employee.

### Performance Pitfalls

> Don't simply complete the performance appraisal form to comply with company policy. The performance appraisal and your meeting time is for your and your employee's benefit and should cover real issues.

To help you plan for the appraisal discussion, we suggest the following steps:

1. Gather documents.
2. Clarify your objectives.
3. Know your employee.
4. Know yourself.
5. Script your discussion.
6. Set employee goals for next period.

7. Determine how much time you'll need to meet.

8. Identify the meeting place.

Let's look at each in a little more detail.

# Gathering Documents

If you have a file for each employee, one where you file all the related documents and materials you may need to reference during the appraisal review meeting, this is the time to pull it out. You should have a copy of the following:

- Your completed appraisal form and written commentary
- A copy of last year's appraisal
- The employee's self-appraisal
- Metrics, if available
- A copy of the employee's job description

If your organization conducts 360-degree feedback exercises, have that information handy, too.

**Performance Pitfalls**

If metrics were used in arriving at the performance rating or level, include those reports in the file. For some positions, this will be the only information used in evaluating performance, and it makes the process highly objective.

Pull from your incident file any appropriate notes, memos, and e-mails dealing with the employee's past performance. Remember that an incident file is more than just a repository of materials documenting adverse performance. It is also a way of retaining documents dealing with exemplary behavior. So remember to revisit times of recognition, memos thanking your employee, certificates of completion for training or educational courses, etc. Your incident file should also contain memory-jogging notes (for you and your employee) dealing with past informal conversations about performance or feedback you gave your employee.

Finally, check your employee's personnel file for any additional documents, records of commendation, warnings, and so forth. You might find company forms and records dealing with new hire information, payroll, employee demographic information, promotion information, transfers, salary increases, training and development, and performance appraisals that can help you evaluate your employee.

 **Performance Pitfalls**

The personnel file should contain only official materials, no copies of memos and e-mails, employee-submitted materials, or anything outside of personnel file policy. Often you hear of an employee asking that something be placed in his personnel file. The employee or manager should keep such information in an incident file.

# Clarifying Your Objectives

What exactly is your objective for the performance discussion with your employee? Is it to communicate total satisfaction with his or her performance? To voice disappointment in his or her not meeting certain performance expectations? Or perhaps it is to be a very detailed discussion about career development, including some personal objectives for the upcoming year. Will it be a difficult meeting where you relay an unsatisfactory evaluation that will require a performance improvement plan? Do you want to focus more on the future than the past by mapping out new goals for your employee? Is it to relay a salary increase?

At every performance review meeting, the manager should have a clear objective. What's yours? As part of the planning process for each and every employee appraisal meeting, write down your main objective(s) and how you intend to achieve (support) those goals. List the points and information you'll bring to the discussion to achieve your objectives. In general, you're going to communicate to your employee how he or she is doing against the job description standards, general performance expectations, and specific goals. You'll be providing dialogue and documents to support your evaluation. It's important to know what objective(s) exist for the meeting and what outcomes you would like to see so you can guide the discussion to those results.

# Considering Your Employee

How well do you know your employee? Given the information and evaluation you're going to convey during your performance meeting, do you know how he or she will react? From our experience, we've found that normally there will be no surprises if both parties follow the process of discussing and setting performance standards, expectations, and goals; complete self-appraisals; and have frequent interaction throughout the year. If expectations are clear, reasonable, achievable, and measurable, the parties can normally arrive at agreement on the work performance.

Still, in some instances, an employee may not agree with the appraisal. He or she may have questions or challenge how you arrived at the assessments and evaluations. You might even receive broad disagreement, anger, and a raised voice. In some cases, the employee won't even respond to the evaluation, refusing to talk about it or even sign the appraisal. In other cases, the employee may burst into tears.

Hopefully, you know your employee and you can, with some certainty, predict how he or she will react to your evaluation, comments, and discussion. Carefully plan for those anticipated reactions as well as the unexpected ones, too. Past behavior is often a predictor of future behavior. If you experienced certain reactions and behaviors with this employee in the past, most likely you will experience it again. Anticipate this.

**Performance Pointers**

See Chapter 3 for information on conducting the appraisal interview.

## Getting to the Root of the Problem

When reviewing areas where the employee fell short of expectations, always take a look at the root cause behind it. Two factors come into play: aptitude and attitude. Your people must have the know-how to do the job: the skills, knowledge, and experience—that's the aptitude. In addition, they must have the right attitude or inclination to want to do their job, and do it right.

It's quite possible that you may view the cause of poor performance to be lack of motivation, when actually it's because the employee was not equipped to do the job. Understand what's truly behind the deficiency before assuming anything. It would be unfortunate to find fault with an employee's performance in a particular area when the individual has the desire and drive to succeed but doesn't have the skills and know-how. Your evaluation will be different, and so should your attitude toward the employee and, ultimately, your solution to the problem.

## Understanding Your Employee's Communication Style

Everyone communicates differently. Knowing how your employees communicate—and how you communicate!—can make performance appraisals easier to deliver and receive. If you've ever been talking with someone and he or she had that "deer in the headlights" look, your message probably wasn't getting through. When you alter your communication style to match your employee's, you have a greater chance that your message, whether positive or constructive criticism, will be fully heard and processed.

There are two ways of acquiring this knowledge: by completing a DISC style assessment or undergoing a Myers-Briggs Type Indicator (MBTI) evaluation. Both are actually personality tests, but they provide insight into behavioral and communication styles and will offer some clues to communicating with your employees.

 **Performance Pointers**

For more information on the Myers-Briggs Type Indicator, or to take the assessment, go to www.myersbriggs.org/. To find out more about the DISC profile, point your browser to www.discprofile.com.

There are four basic personality styles or styles of communicators, and here we give you tips on speaking with each:

- **"A" styles.** *Active, aggressive, achievement-oriented (activity/extroverted).* "A" styles are all business, state issues quickly and factually, and talk about results and achievements. "A"s set high goals.

- **"B" styles.** *Being in the moment, bubbly, bravado, bouncy (people/extroverted).* "B" styles seek opinions and make discussion lively. Be sure recognize them and allow them time to relate and talk. "B"s relate their goals to their dreams and being part of team.

- **"C" styles.** *Cautious, conversational, compliant, careful (people/introverted).* "C" styles are personal and sincere in conversation. When talking to "C"s, listen and respond in soft tones, and don't rush conversation. Give them time to think about the appraisal and new goals.

- **"D" styles.** *Detailed, diligent, data-oriented, deliberate (activity/introverted).* When talking to a "D" style, be prepared and have details about their performance. Be direct yet thoughtful and thorough with "D"s. Be detailed about new goals, dates, and specifics.

You will learn that when you adapt your communication style to your employee's—giving lots of detail to an analytical person, for example, or being

direct with a type "A" person—your message will
be better received. Some people prefer quick,
to-the-point conversations; others require more
time. Some people are change resistant; others
like the excitement of new things. Take time to
master these concepts, and you will be a more
effective leader and communicator.

# Considering Yourself

You need to think about your employee's style, but
you also need to think about your own. Think
about your leadership abilities and limitations,
how you manage time and people, and how you
intend to help your employees succeed in their
jobs and attain their goals.

Part of your appraisal discussion will recap your
employees' responsibilities and specific goals. If
they failed to fulfill certain responsibilities or
complete certain goals, could you or should you
have done something to eliminate the barriers to
your employee's success?

More important, as you set future goals and responsibilities for your people, you must make certain
commitments to enable or empower your employees to achieve those goals. Give some thought
to what your side of the bargain will be so your
employee understands what is expected and how
and where you will (or will not) lend support.
Similarly, what conditions must take place for your
employees to succeed? What information might
they need—external support, budgetary allotments,

knowledge, training, extra hands, time, etc.—to be
successful? Make it clear how you will help and
where they are on their own.

### Performance Pitfalls

> Nothing is more frustrating than for an
> employee to be criticized for not accom-
> plishing an objective when the barrier to
> their accomplishment was you! Just as you
> have expectations of your employees, it's
> reasonable for them to have expectations
> of you.

## Scripting Your Discussion

Yes, you do need to script your appraisal discussion.
Take the time to outline or even write out how you
want the discussion to proceed, step by step. Frame
how the conversation should begin—what you'll
say at the beginning to establish the tone and
intent. Be sure you cover all your points in the
appropriate sequence. You don't have to cover the
appraisal and forms, if you're using them, in a
sequential manner, nor in their totality. Have your
discussion cover the highlights, exceptional performance, any areas where your employee missed
the mark, where improvement is needed, and what
it all means now and going forward.

Take time to review the steps covered in Chapter 3
on how to conduct the performance appraisal, and

use them as talking points during your meeting.
Some managers put the key points on a note card
to reference during the discussion.

# Setting Employee Goals

Although detailed goals don't have to be hammered
out and finalized at this review meeting, a general
discussion of possible employee goals for the next
review period is probably worthwhile. You likely
have a good idea of the personal or soft skill goals
you would like to see your employee work toward.
You also know of company goals for the upcoming
year and your functional goals. It is easy to extrapo-
late these into specific employee goals. Introduce
these during the appraisal discussion, and set a date
to further discuss and solidify them.

# Choosing the Time and Place

Part of the premeeting planning process is assessing
how much time you need to conduct the appraisal
session. No two employees are alike, and performance issues are personal. For some employees,
particularly veterans of the appraisal process or
individuals whose overall performance is fully
acceptable, you won't need much meeting time. If
you've been exchanging feedback throughout the
year, the annual session may require 30 to 45 minutes. For newer employees or ones whose performance is not fully acceptable, you may need more
time. Schedule enough time to accomplish the task.

Put the meeting on your calendar well in advance. Notify your employee of the date, time, and general objective of the session. Remind him or her of things that need to be done prior to the meeting and what to bring to it.

### Performance Pitfalls

Avoid canceling or rescheduling the meeting. This is the most important event of the employee's year; to reschedule it sends a signal that you regard other things as more important. Worse yet, don't tell an employee you have to reschedule because you haven't finished his or her review.

Also give thought to the time of day and week you schedule the meeting. Appraisals that convey primarily positive news can be done any time, any day of the week. Mornings are best because it sets the stage for a great day!

Difficult appraisals, where performance gaps are to be discussed or where disagreement or a bad attitude is anticipated, are best saved for the end of the day or end of the week. This allows the employee to think about it overnight or over the weekend. In fact, you might want to continue the discussion the first thing the next business day. You don't want to relay difficult news and then have the employee return to his or her work area and interact with other employees.

**Performance Pointers** _____

On occasion, you might want to have an HR representative or your own boss sit in with you, particularly if you anticipate problems or major disagreement from your employee. Be sure they are available at the scheduled time.

And it might seem trite, but depending on the nature of the discussion, the physical environment in which you convey the appraisal to your employee can make a world of difference. If you're celebrating an employee's good year of performance, why not truly celebrate it? Take the employee to lunch or dinner for or after the discussion. Some managers prefer to do all their appraisal talks in a neutral place, such as a conference or meeting room. If you choose to use your office, make a decision whether you want it to be a formal setting (for example, at your desk) or in a more relaxed situation away from the desk.

## The Least You Need to Know

- Be sure to gather or request all the necessary documentation you need for the review.
- Before the meeting, make a list of all the points and objectives you need to cover, and sketch out your main points so you know what you're going to say.

- Plan for the unexpected, especially if you think your employee might disagree or get upset with the review.

- Give some thought to when and where to schedule the employee meeting. Time and place can make a difference.

# Chapter 3

# The Meeting

## In This Chapter

- Understanding the purpose of the appraisal meeting
- Exchanging information, ideas, and thoughts
- Handling conflicts
- Following up afterward

The performance appraisal meeting. This is what you've been working up to, and now that you're fully prepared for it—with documentation of how your employee is performing, notes on what you want to say during the meeting, and a pretty good idea of how the meeting will go—you're all set. Assuming you've planned everything beforehand and you've properly informed your employee of how he or she has been doing throughout the year, there should be no surprises for either of you now.

Begin the meeting by making your employee feel as comfortable as possible. You want to create a collaborative environment in which you can have an honest conversation, discuss all the points you've outlined, and answer any questions the employee may have. This is not supposed to be a witch hunt, and if done properly, it won't feel that way to either party. Keep in mind that your subordinate is probably nervous and may be on the defensive. Try to change this by controlling the meeting's pace and environment. A more casual tone will lead to a more productive meeting.

### Performance Pointers

Regardless of your company's process, the meeting is your chance to discuss the information you've collected on your subordinate with him or her. Whether you're required to fill out a summary, use a rank order for each area, or fill in phrases by category, that won't change the protocol for the meeting.

## Yielding Better Results: Collaborative Meetings

After settling in, review the goals set for your subordinate for the past year. We suggest reviewing each goal or point of discussion separately and asking questions about it. How does your employee think he or she did compared to each goal? How could the employee have improved? What tools, resources, training, or other things would have helped the employee do better? Only after discussing each point through questions should you give your employee your take on how he or she did.

It's rare that you will both have the exact same take on each issue. Often people are more critical of themselves than others—including their manager—might be. Discuss both takes openly. Your employee may be able to provide additional information you weren't aware of. The employee might have had some unseen barriers to success. If you can't reach a consensus on one or more points, agree to disagree and leave it at that. After a while, there is no longer any benefit of continuing that part of the conversation.

 **Performance Pointers**

With their direct experience, your employees may be able to provide valuable insight into how they and their peers can produce more in the future.

# Dealing With Disagreements

Disagreements usually stem from a lack of proper understanding between you and your subordinate. You need to look into several areas when disagreements occur:

- Did you and your subordinate have the same understanding of the employee's responsibilities?

- Were there extenuating circumstances?
- Did he or she have all the tools and training required to succeed?
- Did the employee misunderstand the goals of his or her assignments?

Whatever the root of the disagreement, the performance review is an excellent opportunity for you to clarify your goals and expectations and set your employee off on the right track to improve. It's essential to figure out where the differences are, discuss the issues, and assure your subordinate that he or she is now armed with all the right information needed to show improvement during the next review.

 **Performance Pointers**

When a disagreement arises, be certain to document both sides in an objective fashion. Try to list facts and areas of disagreement without an emotional skew. This documentation will prove invaluable should the same kinds of disagreements occur in the next performance review.

In some cases, a subordinate might become overly emotional and react with some inappropriate behavior. Any kind of yelling, use of profanity, crying, threats, ultimatums, etc. are not to be accepted under any circumstances. Although you might understand the frustration, these kind of outbursts cannot lead to a productive resolution. In some cases, if you simply ask the subordinate if he or she would like to continue the discussion at a later time when he or she has regained composure, the subordinate will straighten up. If this kind of behavior continues, ask this person to leave your office immediately.

We have to emphasize that if you ever feel physically intimidated by someone you're reviewing, do not hesitate to take action. You should immediately change the situation to a safer one. Ask the person to leave your office, leave the office yourself, or call security. There's absolutely no shame in dealing with a bully. Your safety and that of your co-workers comes first and foremost.

## Ending the Meeting

After the issues have been discussed and both sides have communicated, don't let the meeting drag on. After a certain amount of discussion, you reach a point of diminishing returns. Beyond that, the meeting can become counterproductive. Before you get to this point, summarize the meeting and all the points covered, set the stage for the follow-up meeting, and inform the subordinate that the meeting is over for the day.

## Deciding on Post-Meeting Action

After an appraisal, there has to be a resulting course of action. For a poor performer, you need to be sure this person had the necessary tools, training, and resources necessary for success. Assuming this subordinate had everything he or she needed to succeed, you then have to design a work improvement plan. This plan should include new goals along with a new set of the absolute minimum expectations the employee must meet to remain in the position. These goals and minimums should be created for weekly or monthly progress, depending on the type of position. Each week or month, depending on which timescale you've selected, meet with your employee to review progress. Doing so will give you the opportunity to coach the employee and thus provide the best chance of success.

 **Performance Pointers**

When setting employee goals, be sure to make them **S.M.A.R.T.**:

- **S**pecific
- **M**easurable
- **A**ttainable
- **R**elative and realistic
- **T**ime-based

The moderate performer, similar to the poor performer, may not have had the necessary tools, training, and resources necessary to achieve more. If the moderate performer does have everything needed to achieve more, a work improvement plan may be appropriate. With adjusted goals and regular coaching sessions, this moderate performer may just become a top performer.

Most managers overlook the top performers. They believe that whatever these individuals are doing works and often fear that any interference may hurt performance or cause them to become dissatisfied with their job and potentially leave. What such managers don't realize, however, is that these top people are the ones who are the most motivated and eager to perform even better. If you overlook these employees, you run the greatest risk of losing them. Once again, training, coaching, and raising the bar can be invaluable to help these subordinates do even better than the excellent job they are currently doing. Everyone has room for improvement, even the cream of the crop.

## The Least You Need to Know

- During the performance appraisal meeting, create a collaborative environment so employees won't be defensive and will share valuable information with you.
- Be prepared for anything. Emotions can run high during an appraisal.
- After the meeting, you need to set a course of action—for poor performers as well as those employees who excel in their position.
- Don't overlook the top performers. They also crave coaching, and it can benefit them enormously.

# 2

## What to Say: Phrases

Stuck for how to say an employee needs to step up and work on his or her leadership skills? Need to share with an employee that he or she needs to improve his or her interpersonal skills—whether with clients or peers? Want to remind an employee that their desk isn't, in fact, a black hole for files and reports? Want to praise an employee for doing such a good job without sounding flowery or exaggerated?

If you need to comment on any of these situations, you've come to the right part of the book.

# General Phrases by Attribute: A–B

Often, when writing out a performance appraisal, it's easy to experience writer's block when trying to find just the right phrases to describe an employee. The job description provides ample language and information for describing specific work-related duties and tasks, but what about the important soft skills the employee must exhibit? How do you write about strengths and deficiencies in these areas?

The following phrases represent some of the more important personal traits that may be important to cover in an employee's appraisal. This list just scratches the surface, but it will surely jump-start your thoughts and help you zero in on exactly what you want to say.

## Accuracy

Accuracy deals with how careful and exacting one is with his or her work content and output. Accurate work is work significantly free of errors and very precise.

### Positive Phrases

Work delivered virtually error free

Has a very low error rate *(cite data)*

Carefully proofs work before handing it in

Uses spell-checker effectively

Is an excellent proofreader

Catches all mistakes

Gets it right the first time

Is detail-oriented

Is committed to a high degree of accuracy

Seeks out colleagues to edit work

Strives for perfection

Delivers assignments without flaws

Is respected for being accurate with work

Rarely allows oversights

Seeks perfection

Double-checks work before sending it out

Understands the importance of work being precise

Never omits information

## Negative Phrases

Makes mistakes frequently

Resists having work checked

Does not adhere to proscribed standards

Rushes with work, creating errors

Is careless with work

Often omits important information

Is lax in proofing work

Does not verify data used in reports

Does not check work

Overlooks details in job

Is imprecise with calculations and forecasts

Launches into work unprepared

## Adaptability

Adaptability is being able to adjust to changing situations; new work; last-minute requests; and new priorities, directions, and approaches. When people are rigid and resist changes, you can help by painting a picture of how both the person and company will benefit from the change. Remember, however, that in the end, the person has to buy into the change.

### Positive Phrases

Is able to perform many different functions

Is cross-trained

Can grow with the job

Handles new tasks

Is very flexible with priorities

Wears many hats

Learns new skills quickly

Is able to transfer skills

Has breadth of knowledge beyond current needs

Is highly versatile

Is multitalented

Deals well with a changing environment

Is a quick study with new projects

Is adept at multitasking

Is highly adaptable

Is able to identify and adjust to new situations

Reacts positively to sudden requests

Is open to change

Performs a number of different roles

Pitches in where needed

## Negative Phrases

Resists changes in work procedures

Last-minute changes create stress

Complains about changes in work

Can't start new project or work assignment until first one is done

Cannot handle two tasks at the same time

Prefers to work on activities that are familiar or repetitive

Becomes flustered when asked to do things differently

Is reluctant to drop current project and take on new work

Takes too long when taking on new work

Is very rigid in approach to work

Is reluctant to take suggestions from others

Wants to always do it the "old way"

Does not like changes in the middle of a project

## Analytical Skills

An employee who has strong analytical skills knows how to take a problem or task, break it down into parts, analyze the parts, and solve the problem.

### Positive Phrases

Comprehends complex issues

Finds accurate comparables

Solves problems methodically

Breaks down the whole into its constituent components

Is very detailed with analysis

Anticipates problems based on data available

Makes logical conclusions

Understands the function of each individual element

Approaches problems methodically

Shows insight when dealing with data

Reviews data systematically

Is able to observe differences in similar items

Has excellent analytical skills

Locates problems in complex systems

Has insight into numbers

Is very method-oriented in approach to problem-solving

Draws excellent conclusions from information at hand

Is always curious and seeking new solutions

## Negative Phrases

Doesn't utilize tools and processes to secure answers

Doesn't stay abreast of new analytical methods

Does not keep up-to-date with analytical methods

Doesn't utilize all information available

Tends to be overwhelmed by large amounts of information

Puts little thought into analysis of data

Takes too much time when analyzing a problem

Needs to think more outside the box when approaching new challenges

Has not developed a consistent approach to analytics

# Appearance

Appearance is how one presents oneself, his or her clothing and grooming, either at work or while on business. An employee's appearance is a reflection on himself as well as the company he or she represents.

## Positive Phrases

Dresses professionally

Is particular about appearance

Always inquires about client dress code before visiting

Is proud of his or her appearance

Makes a point of always dressing tastefully

Sets the standard for business casual clothing

Keeps company uniform clean

Wears stylish clothes that enhance image

Takes the time to make self ready for work

Has a businesslike look

Maintains a neat and orderly appearance

Never neglects to wear uniform

## Negative Phrases

Does not always adhere to company dress code

Cannot be relied upon to dress appropriately for guests

Colleagues have complained about personal grooming

Resists suggestions about improvements to dress and grooming

Has embarrassed company at offsite meetings with appearance

Needs to pay more attention to personal hygiene

## Aptitude

Aptitude is the ability to learn or understand. Often it is seen as a natural ability or talent. Because it is a natural propensity, these innate abilities cannot be learned, changed, exchanged, or developed.

## Positive Phrases

Has a natural talent in this field

Grasps challenges at hand

Tends to understand easily

Shows potential with new projects

Is a gifted person in this area

## Aptitude *continued*

Has a flair for this field

Requires little time to come up to speed

Is facile with new situations

Is well suited for the job

Learns quickly and retains knowledge

Is a quick study

Has good instincts about his or her job

Has a knack for the job

Does not require repetition to master new skills

## Negative Phrases

Does not always understand tasks assigned

Takes too long to understand assignment

Doesn't always grab hold of the basics

Must do new work many times over before getting it down

Is slow to start new work

Requires repeated training on the same issues

Needs help with learning new processes

# Attendance and Punctuality

Attendance is the regularity with which an employee comes to work, being there and being on time for work and for appointments or meetings. Punctuality is key in many industries, and only helps make an employee get off to a good start.

## Positive Phrases

Frequently shows up for work early

Always arrives on time

Is never late to meetings

Often stays after hours

Can be relied on to be on time

Arrives early for appointments

Never misses work unexpectedly

Hands in assignments on time

Leaves for the day only after work is completed

Only calls in sick when absolutely necessary

Never requires reminders about meetings

Uses discretion with company sick days

Prides self on attendance record

Calls ahead when delayed or going to be late

Is always punctual

# Attendance and Punctuality
*continued*

Groups personal appointments so as to not miss much time

Takes fewer breaks than allocated

Finishes assignments before leaving work for the day

## Negative Phrases

Is not predictable nor reliable with attendance

Always makes excuses for being late

Has tendency to watch the clock

Underestimates driving time

Takes personal time in excess of policy

Fails to call in when there's a problem

Needs help with time management

Doesn't seem to care about being on time for work

Is habitually late

Leaves work early

Returns from breaks after designated time

# Attitude

Your employee can have all the latest skills, training, and experience, but if his or her attitude—his or her frame of mind or mental approach to work—is anything less than positive, the job will not get done in a satisfactory manner, and the person's negativity could spill over to other employees. If this is the case, you need to address it in the appraisal and demand a change.

## Positive Phrases

Is enthusiastic about work

Is energetic and lively

Never makes waves

Has positive outlook

Has a "can do" approach

Is excited to get to work

Values his or her job

Takes feedback well

Takes work seriously

Deals with others in a patient manner

Has realistic outlook about work

Rarely complains

Is never subjective with thinking

## Attitude *continued*

Accepts constructive criticism

Takes on work beyond his or her job duties

Works well with others

Wants to satisfy customers

Enjoys challenges

### Negative Phrases

Doesn't always believe in self

Rarely offers help to others

Is not a team player

Does not accepts responsibility

Is often negative in comments about company

Sells self short on job

Is condescending to others

Is critical of others

Has an attitude of entitlement

Does not seem to want to work hard

Is not interested in improvement

Tends to be overconfident about abilities

Allows others to influence his or her thinking

# Behavior

Behavior is the manner or way a person conducts him- or herself. It's how one acts in the presence of others.

## Positive Phrases

Acts appropriately for work

Does not engage in company politics

Avoids unnecessary conversations with peers

Handles customers well

Greets others in a proper manner

Does not panic

Is sensitive to the feelings of others

Respects others' opinions and inputs

Proceeds in a professional manner

Is very ethical in behavior

Does not engage in antics of his or her peers

Avoids inappropriate confrontations

Maintains a businesslike style

Is a role model for new employees

Steers clear of others who act inappropriately at work

Looks others in the eyes when speaking with them

## Behavior *continued*

### Negative Phrases

Tends not to take work seriously

Does not handle adverse or stressful situations well

Doesn't know when to stop talking

Cannot be counted on with clients

Has tendency to belittle work associates

Allows personal feelings to get in the way of work relationships

Actions do not always mirror intent

Interrupts others in meetings

Needs to watch language in front of others

Has been known to insult others

Attitude gets in the way of getting work done

## Business Ethics

This subject addresses one's conformance to acceptable morals and business standards of conduct. This includes such areas as fair play, honesty, moral duty, and loyalty.

## Positive Phrases

Is honest beyond repute

Has an excellent reputation

Is well thought of

Has never omitted the truth

Deals with others in a fair and equal manner

Upholds company policy

Is highly ethical

Always follows company policy

High ethics makes for a company role model

Is compassionate toward others

Abhors dishonesty

Steps forward when he or she has made an error

Admits when he or she is wrong

Is sensitive to cultural and racial differences

Reports discrepancies immediately

Consults others when uncertain about course of action

Gives credit to deserved parties

Handles disputes impartially

Gets the proper authorization

## Business Ethics *continued*

Is a moral compass for fellow employees

Is conservative with company's money

Removes self from decisions when he or she lacks objectivity

### Negative Phrases

Sidesteps company procedures and policies

Fails to take responsibility for his or her mistakes

Is not truthful and forthcoming

Has a tendency to exaggerate

Sometimes cuts corners

Is regarded as untrustworthy

Word is not always good

Blames others for mistakes

Hides his or her mistakes from supervisor

Is reluctant to admit when wrong

Uses questionable methods to get job done

# Chapter 5

# General Phrases by Attribute: C–F

A specific employee's job and performance are almost always directly tied to those of other employees on his or her team, outside vendors, and their network at large. One of your objectives in the performance appraisal process is to isolate the individual's performance from all the surrounding support structures. This can be a difficult task. Keep in mind, when evaluating more than one person with the same responsibilities, that they may have outside factors affecting their performance. These factors need to be taken into account when you are making the evaluation.

# Communication—Oral

Communication skills are critical in today's workplace. One must be able to be clear and crisp with oral and written communications. If you have someone lacking in those areas, put together a developmental or action plan that requires attending a writing course or public speaking.

## Positive Phrases

Speaks articulately

Speaks in a short, concise manner

Is always understood

Has a robust vocabulary

Allows other people to speak

Thinks before speaking

Is good at asking clarifying questions

Knows when to be firm of voice

Is never at a loss for words

Has excellent presentation skills

Always watches others to be sure his or her message is understood when presenting

Presents thoughts in words easily understood by the listener

Is a good spokesperson for departmental meetings

Is unflappable in front of the press and media

Is not intimidated by audiences

Speaks up immediately

Has good telephone manners

Is careful in explanation to others

Is an accomplished speaker

Uses words well to illustrate points

Uses appropriate words

Is good at reading body language

Understands needs of others and communicates appropriately

Follows up to be sure message is understood

Does not hide bad news

Understands technical jargon

Keeps the appropriate people informed

Consistently gets his or her point across

Speaks magnificently

Is excellent at translating _____

## Negative Phrases

Talks too loudly/talks too softly

Often dominates conversation

Gets flustered when asked to speak before groups

Always summarizes what he or she said

## Communication—Oral *continued*

Fails to encourage questions

Doesn't allow others to finish what they have
to say

Is not organized with thoughts

Has a tendency to repeat

Talks too fast, thus losing people

Needs to talk faster and in shorter sentences

Uses argumentative tone of voice

Rambles too much

Tries to impress listener with big words

Becomes intimidated when interrupted

Needs to be more succinct

## Communication—Written

In this age of e-mails and text messages, sometimes
written communication—conveyance of information—via the written word—is unfortunately tossed
to the wayside. But just because you *can* send an
all-lowercase e-mail to your co-worker or use slang
and fragments doesn't mean you *should.*

### Positive Phrases

Writes effectively

Has excellent editing skills

Uses e-mail appropriately

Is organized with slides

Is an excellent writer

Writes with reader in mind

Uses vocabulary everyone can understand

Checks spelling for accuracy

Follows formatting guidelines

Proofreads work before sending it out

Augments with visual aids

Uses concise language

Uses proper grammar

Has an excellent command of English

Can summarize information in a minimum of
words

## Negative Phrases

Lacks good sentence structure

Translates inaccurately

Corresponds poorly

Is wordy

Is ineffective in written communications

Often repeats material

Has a tendency to show off with big words

## Communication–Written *continued*

Runs sentences together often

Writes without thinking

Doesn't proofread work

Grammar needs improvement

Uses inappropriate words

Needs to work on tone and style

Work contains spelling errors

Needs to utilize spell-checker to ensure accuracy

## Conflict Management

Conflict management is the ability to handle disagreements and end disputes. It requires the ability to see both sides of the problem and find common ground for the people involved.

### Positive Phrases

Settles disputes

Finds common ground

Understands both sides of the argument

Gets concessions from each party

Creates a collaborative environment

Opens the channels of communication

Creates win-win solutions

Gets to the facts

Eliminates ego factor on both sides

Suggests alternatives

Gets through to the real decision-makers

Keeps the ultimate goal in mind

Helps others see the ultimate goal

Asks questions to uncover information

Prevents escalation

Defuses difficult situations

Breaks deadlocks

## Negative Phrases

Escalates issues

Offends others

Only sees one side of the disagreement

Wants to win at all costs

Refuses any alternatives

Is unwilling to compromise on any points

Lets other issues get in the way

Has an attitude of entitlement

Comes off as arrogant

## Conflict Management *continued*

Throws tantrums

Fires vendors instead of dealing with the issues

Avoids conflict altogether

Holds grudges and takes issues personally

Adds fuel to arguments

## Cost-Consciousness

Cost-consciousness is an essential for any employee with budgetary responsibility. A cost-conscious employee can do more with less money, increase efficiency, and reduce costs.

Although cost-consciousness is especially important for employees with budgets, at all levels, employees can be encouraged to make suggestions that will cut costs without reducing quality or productivity.

### Positive Phrases

Increases departmental productivity

Adds value to existing lines

Designs cost-saving systems

Generates cost-cutting ideas

Purchases efficiently

Chooses cost-efficient suppliers

Establishes acquisition procedures

Implements efficiency training programs

Reduces redundancies

Negotiates bulk rates with vendors

Gets multiple quotes prior to purchasing

Finds more competitive vendors than those currently used

Suggests bidding-process enhancements

Gets discounts for combined purchases

Procures goods and services through barter

Reduces headcount while maintaining production

Finds ways to cut costs

Outsources nonessential functions

## Negative Phrases

Increases costs

Insists on new resources without justification

Gets few bids

Uses obsolete technology

Grants contracts based on relationships and not cost

Increases headcount

Adds administrative work, which reduces productivity

Needs more resources than his or her peers to do the same job

## Cost-Consciousness *continued*

Buys impulsively

Employs the newest technology even when impractical

Does not contain costs

Wastes resources

## Creativity

Creativity is the ability to find new approaches, ideas, solutions, or methods. Only with a full knowledge of available technologies, processes, and materials can an individual effectively come up with alternative solutions.

### Positive Phrases

Comes up with new ways to handle issues

Finds innovative solutions to problems

Conceptualizes well

Is an excellent problem-solver

Improves existing systems

Develops solutions

Finds answers in nontraditional sources

Has an unorthodox approach

Thinks outside the box

Finds new configurations

Shapes existing programs

Finds new resources

Finds solutions

Is highly creative

Thinks of new ideas

Makes new suggestions

## Negative Phrases

Uses old approaches

Is not creative

Does not invent new techniques

Lacks creative flair

Is unable to be imaginative

Is not inventive

Uses unimaginative processes

Has no vision for new ideas

Employs unoriginal approaches

Has difficulty creating new methods

Cannot find solutions

Is unable to conceptualize

Does not generate anything new

Produces stale ideas and materials

## Customer Focus

Customer focus means putting the customer's needs first. It goes beyond customer services to ensure customer satisfaction at every level.

### Positive Phrases

Communicates thoughtfully

Knows who the customer is

Seeks to satisfy end user in a reasonable manner

Is helpful in assisting clients

Offers help

Educates customers

Seeks mutually beneficial solutions

Builds relationships with customers

Helps customers understand their needs

Retains customers

Is excellent at dealing with emotional customers

Provides product support

Strives for value-added solutions

Is attentive to customers' needs

Exhibits tact and professionalism with customers

Doesn't overpromise

Is eager to please

Gives service with a smile

Helps customers beyond requirements

Greets customers by name

Offers customers expert advice when asked

Is expedient with solutions for customers

Asks customers about additional needs

Thanks customers for their business

Asks customers for ways to improve service

## Negative Phrases

Dumps calls that aren't directly related to function

Is rude with customers

Rarely gives assistance

Is solely focused on direct responsibilities

Is slow to offer customer assistance

Ignores customers' additional needs

Does not ask customers about their additional needs

Is unapproachable to customers

Makes self unavailable to customers

Looks unhappy when asked for help

## Customer Focus *continued*

Acts as if customers are burdens

Makes customers feel unwelcome

Makes customers feel unimportant

Looks down on customers

Is reluctant to assist customers

Treats customers with distain

Frequently corrects customers

Is insulting toward customers

Exhibits anti-customer sentiment

## Decision-Making

Decision-making is the act of making the best decision possible with the information available. This can include the decision that more information must be gathered before a decision is made. Not making a decision is also considered a decision.

### Positive Phrases

Makes sound decisions

Weighs options before deciding on the correct course of action

Makes unpopular decisions when necessary

Makes decisions quickly when necessary

Makes decisions based on facts

Researches possible results before making decisions

Considers alternative approaches

Consults with experts before taking action

Weighs potential consequences

Uses all available resources within reason

Is willing to make tough or unpleasant decisions

Involves others when appropriate

Stands up for his or her decisions

Does not allow emotions to play a part in decision-making

Is willing to make new decisions as more information becomes available

Is able to make decisions

## Negative Phrases

Is unable to make decisions

Never has enough information prior to making decisions

Is indecisive

Vacillates between decisions

Hesitates when immediate decisions are required

Overanalyzes and makes slow decisions

Involves others in decisions when inappropriate

## Decision-Making *continued*

Relies on gut rather than facts

Uses experts with wrong expertise when making decisions

Makes poor decisions

Makes rash decisions

Finds excuses for decisions made

Asks others to make decisions

Makes decisions based on nonfacts

## Delegation

Delegation is the ability to assign appropriate tasks to others to maximize work output. It's a difficult balancing act, though. Although it's essential to delegate to maximize productivity, overdelegation can decrease quality or control. For maximum efficiency, it's best to delegate to the lowest possible level.

### Positive Phrases

Gives subordinates appropriate assignments

Delegates based on individual skills and abilities of employees

Delegates to the lowest possible level

Empowers employees

Trains employees to handle new tasks

Instills confidence in others

Motivates others to succeed at new tasks

Retains mission-critical assignments for self

Does not overdelegate

Gives subordinates proper authority to complete
tasks

Takes responsibility for delegated tasks

Welcomes recommendations

Checks over work when appropriate

Evaluates workload and redistributes as needed

Monitors progress through weekly reports

Learns from peers what they delegate and how

Sets realistic deadlines

Identifies responsibilities that can be handed off

## Negative Phrases

Delegates mission-critical tasks

Poorly trains people to whom tasks are delegated

Delegates tasks unevenly

Does everything himself or herself

Is afraid to lose control

Won't hand off assignments

## Delegation *continued*

Overdelegates

Does not motivate employees to take pride in delegated tasks

Does not set deadlines for projects to be completed

Sets deadlines that are impossible to achieve

Micromanages projects

Passes blame on to subordinates

Does not proof, edit, and correct delegated assignments

Does not review needs for delegated project

Is unavailable to subordinates who are working on tasks

Is unwilling to explain new methods to subordinates

Does not train employees to take on new tasks

Delegates to inappropriate personnel

## Dependability

Dependability is characterized by a history of consistent reliability. Dependability can only be established by an individual's track record. This may not be an appropriate area to evaluate a new employee due to their short history with the company.

## Positive Phrases

Is highly reliable

Follows through on assignments

Consistently delivers

Follows the plan

Can be relied upon

Stays on budget

Meets all deadlines

Does what is necessary to complete projects

Follows up when appropriate

Can be depended on

Always follows through

Delivers more than the required minimum

Comes through for the customer

Always keeps promises

Exceeds expectations

## Negative Phrases

Is not reliable

Is reliable only some of the time

Doesn't always follow through

Makes but doesn't keep promises

## Dependability *continued*

Rarely meets goals

Achieves inconsistently

Fails to finish tasks

Completes tasks after deadline has passed

Does not maintain records as agreed upon

Does not follow directions

Turns in assignments with flaws

Hands in forms late

Does not follow up on projects

Shows up for work at incorrect times

Fails to show up for work with no apparent reason

## Financial Management

Financial management involves overseeing monetary resources and related accounting issues and sticking to a budget. This might not apply to all employees, but because companies exist to make money, this is an important area for review.

### Positive Phrases

Sets challenging financial goals

Reduces costs

Increases productivity

Finds ways to increase revenue

Adds more value to products than competitors

Justifies capital expenditures

Closes the books in a timely fashion

Recognizes the importance of strict financial management

Sticks to the budget

Delivers projects on time

Reduces overhead

Carefully manages inventory levels

Looks for breakthrough opportunities

Works with accounting experts for new ideas

Looks carefully into expenditures

Signs off on all expenses personally

Involves staff in budget process

Eliminates vendors when appropriate

## Negative Phrases

Sets sloppy budgets

Has too many miscellaneous costs in budget

Does not look into all costs

Does not spot irregularities

Inadequately handles receivables

# Financial Management *continued*

Generates imprecise reports

Has no departmental financial goals

Is unable to meet budgets

Hands over too much financial control

Is unable to cut costs

Has unacceptable inventory/turn ratio

Does not get proper backup prior to paying invoices

Records transactions improperly

Is too highly leveraged

Does not utilize resources to their full extent

Reduces profit

Increases financial risk and exposure

Is unable to diversify investments

# Fit Within Organization

Every company or organization has a corporate culture. An employee's individual ideas, philosophies, and even look need to match that of the institution for a smooth-running company.

Despite knowledge, hard work, technical skills, and other important attributes, new employees often fail because they're a poor fit for the organization. This creates an unhealthy environment and must be corrected immediately. Ignoring the problem will generally only make matters worse.

## Positive Phrases

Works well with peers

Is well respected

Is well liked

Dresses in a way that is consistent with the company format

Has neat and tidy appearance

Has goals in common with the company

Wants to see others succeed

Uses internal resources effectively

Understands and avoids company politics

Agrees with company procedures

Understands company guidelines

Effectively utilizes manager's time

Is open to learning new processes

Likes to learn new methods of performing tasks

Rarely questions authorities

Is supportive of company directives

Believes in the company's mission

# Fit Within Organization *continued*

Is passionate about the company's products and services

Is receptive to change

Completes assignments gladly

## Negative Phrases

Has own ideas of how things should work

Does not trust manager's judgment

Questions new directives

Uses nonstandard methods

Violates company procedures

Dresses in an inappropriately casual manner

Does not support company's mission statement

Feels that company's direction is not the right one

Wants to develop his or her own processes

Has preconceived ideas of how the company should be run

Has values not aligned with the company's

Questions authority frequently

Openly disagrees with policies

Refuses to sign employment documents

Is unwilling to adhere to guidelines

Questions manager in front of others

Does not believe in company's products

Feels company adds little value

Finds pricing model unrealistic

Engages in office politics

Goes over people's heads

Frequently quarrels with others

Does not get proper authorization

# Flexibility

Flexibility is the capability to perform a variety of different tasks or functions. It involves both the technical know-how and the willingness to perform these duties. Flexibility is also the ability to change and adapt as needed.

## Positive Phrases

Is open to new approaches

Is receptive to others' suggestions

Is willing to work additional hours

Tries to accommodate last-minute schedule changes

Is able to change tasks depending on manager's needs

## Flexibility *continued*

Searches for alternative and new solutions

Can be counted on to pick up where others left off

Adapts work schedule to meet department needs

Embraces changes in job responsibilities

Is highly flexible in work routine

Overcomes obstacles to change

Has an open mind

Is cross-trained

Learns new functions to provide backup when needed

Has knowledge in a variety of areas that exceeds his or her duties

Enjoys the uncertainty of the workday

Is willing to take on additional responsibilities when necessary

Responds to possibilities

### Negative Phrases

Is unwilling to change

Will not try new approaches

Does not consider alternate methods

Considers everything non-negotiable

Is highly specialized

Is unwilling to pitch in where needed

Is unable to learn new skills outside his or her
area of expertise

Is inflexible

Will not deviate from daily routine

Does not understand new ideas

Is reluctant to try new things

Is adverse to change

Will not consider suggestions

Only uses one approach

# Follow-Through

Employees with good follow-through see an assignment through completion and monitor its progress
beyond to ensure its success. Good follow-through
requires good planning and organization skills.

## Positive Phrases

Responds to others at the agreed-upon time

Utilizes an electronic calendar to manage obliga-
tions

Can be relied upon to follow up on action items

Never needs to be reminded to follow up

## Follow-Through *continued*

Completes assignments on time

Does what he or she says will be done

Establishes doable targets and completes them on time

Is well organized with future commitments

Double-checks with others' action expectations and deadlines

Is very detailed with dates and reminders

Never misses agreed-upon appointment

Gets to work on new projects immediately after assignment

Clarifies next steps and dates after assignment is handed off

Completes tasks thoroughly

Does not lose sight of project after it is handed off

Follows assignments through to completion

Finishes one task before starting another

Follows progress after assignment is handed off

### Negative Phrases

Finishes only 90 percent of his or her work

Does not complete assignments

Completes assignments well after deadlines have expired

Starts projects but does not see them through

Takes on too many tasks and is unable to complete them all

Does not follow up on agreed-upon times

Loses sight of project after handed off

Gets distracted and forgets about assignments

Starts new projects before completing existing tasks

Tries to take on multiple tasks simultaneously

# General Phrases by Attribute: G–N

When giving or writing a performance appraisal, it's important to always back your phrases with examples. There's nothing worse than relaying a negative comment without having specifics to show as examples. The same goes for positive statements. Be sure you can relay situations that reinforce the performance descriptors. For appraisals to be useful and effective, they must be objective, consistent, fair, and defensible. Failing to do this can ultimately lead to a system that demoralizes employees instead of empowering them to improve. This empowerment can be a powerful motivator and a tool to help employees value the performance appraisal process.

# General Job Skills

Every employee has some general job skills in addition to his or her job-specific instruction and education. General job skills are the overall skills necessary to satisfactorily perform a job. It's the basic know-how to get the job done.

## Positive Phrases

Fully trained on current job

Has excellent knowledge of job

Utilizes knowledge from all areas

Has superb soft skills

Makes use of industry knowledge

Always looking for new information

Constantly improving job know-how

Brings strong past experience to the job

Stays current with the technology

Maximizes use of computer and software applications

Knows how to apply knowledge to job

Always proactive in job

Is a rounded individual who leverages information and contacts

Involves others in solution when the answer isn't evident

## Negative Phrases

Does not stay current with job know-how

Possesses the skills to do job but not the drive

Lacks all the necessary skills to do the job

Requires remedial training

Is reluctant to take outside courses to improve skills

Resists coaching on job know-how

Is held back by marginal computer skills

Is not fully competent

Needs to stay on top of new technologies

Is hesitant to broaden job knowledge

Tries to do job with obsolete skills

# Giving and Receiving Feedback

Although some employees request feedback and others would not hear how they're doing, feedback is an important element of any job's success. The employee must be willing to receive feedback, and the manager must be good at providing it.

## Positive Phrases

Very receptive to suggestions and ideas of others

Has a knack for giving feedback

Provides meaningful feedback

## Giving and Receiving Feedback
*continued*

Constantly asks for feedback and suggestions

Is a role model for sharing feedback

Incorporates feedback into work

Proactively seeks feedback

Offers meaningful constructive criticism

Documents employee performance and offers improvement ideas

Seeks feedback when having difficulty doing job

Is one of the best job coaches in company

Has unique ability to assess performance

Embraces feedback and uses it where appropriate

Proactively seeks out boss for feedback

Is tactful in giving feedback

Gives useful and motivating feedback

Provides good mix of positive and developmental feedback

Makes excellent use of feedback

### Negative Phrases

Is reluctant to offer feedback to employees

Shies from giving feedback when it creates conflict

Is not receptive to manager's suggestions

Does poor job of providing feedback

Doesn't make good use of feedback received

Lacks interpersonal skills to provide feedback

Is argumentative when help is offered

Never requests feedback on how he or she is doing in job

Will not listen to others

Gives thoughtless and insensitive feedback

Gives inconsistent feedback

Is overly detailed with personal advice

Never offers complimentary feedback

Doesn't take advantage of feedback received

## Improvement

Improvement is about doing one's job better, about striving to get better in their position with the help of more knowledge, time spent, updated processes, better results, etc.

### Positive Phrases

Always looking for ways to improve performance

Excellent at root cause analysis to solve problems

Correctly applies Six Sigma tools to improve process

## Improvement *continued*

Solicits suggestions of others to improve work

Uses process mapping to streamline operation

Looks for small ways to make a difference

Is a big-picture person whose ideas become improvement actions

Does not give up on finding new ways to do things

Encourages others to do things better

Uses metrics to document improvements

Creates a positive environment for work ideas

Always pushes self to personally improve

Takes relevant night courses

Continually learns new methods

Constantly reads new business books and applies ideas

Completed Kaizen training and began using in department

### Negative Phrases

Does not study processes

Rarely makes suggestions to benefit team

Does not take courses

Refuses to read new training materials

Prefers to perform tasks as they have always been done

Needs to gain new skills

Does not have any interest in industry journals

Avoids industry training

Does not see the value in new skills

Is adverse to change

Feels he or she cannot make a difference

Is not motivated to make a difference

Would benefit from watching top-performing peers

Needs to invest in self

Is not interested in improving in job

Resists opportunities to learn more

Is declining in job output

Does not stay abreast of new methods

Sees no value in applying process improvement tools

Fails to see need for improvement

Is unresponsive to suggestions for improving performance

Sees no further improvement possible without outside course work

Does not believe additional improvement is possible

# Independence/Autonomy

Some employees almost need their manager to outline specifically what they need to do. Others can
pick up a project and work on it without a lot of
managerial supervision. Being able to work inde-
pendently or with autonomy means working with
little management or outside assistance.

## Positive Phrases

Works well on his or her own

Needs very little direction

Completes projects with minimal assistance

Needs very few outside resources

Figures out things on his or her own

Fixes problems with no outside help

Can be relied upon to deliver on time with minimal management

Does not need reminders to complete tasks

Requires minimal supervision

Is self-managing

Does not require others to review work

Deals with conflicts without assistance

## Negative Phrases

Needs constant direction

Has questions about things that should be known

Needs intense management

Cannot remember to complete tasks on his or her own

Requires tremendous outside resources

Gets easily distracted when working on his or her own

Is not able to complete tasks without help

Needs to be shown everything

Is unable to figure out things on his or her own

Has to be taught the same thing multiple times

Cannot memorize tasks

Constantly needs to discuss issues with manager

Requires help in difficult situations

## Initiative

Initiative means taking the bull by the horns and getting things done without being asked to do so. It requires independence, but it also requires that the person have enough job knowledge and self-esteem to know they can get the job done.

## Initiative *continued*

### Positive Phrases

Is a true self-starter

Is very proactive when problems surface

Anticipates what must be done

Highly independent and reliable

Always know work is getting done without asking

Never needs reminders

Is always on top of the situation

Knows how to pull people together and tackle the
work at hand

Presses others to action

Is usually the first to get started and to finish

Immediately tackles tough assignments

Requires little management

Needs direction infrequently

Never waits to be told; knows what to do and
does it

Is timely in launching new projects

### Negative Phrases

Feels the need for approval before beginning

Needs to be asked to do each assignment

Does not anticipate needs

Starts later than others

Waits to be told what needs to be done

Does not rely on own expertise

Stops in the middle of projects to wait for review

Waits for review of finished assignments before beginning others

Hesitates when making a decision

Is unable to make decisions without management present

Asks questions to which he or she knows the answer

# Innovation

Innovation is the act of creating unusual or unorthodox solutions to problems. It requires resourcefulness and a lot of thinking outside the box.

## Positive Phrases

Is constantly thinking of new ideas

Is a creative thinker who can translate ideas into products

Asks others for suggestions

An excellent brainstormer

## Innovation *continued*

Enjoys the challenge of doing things in new and better ways

Pushes department to think outside the box

Uses process improvement tools to create innovation

Thinks in unorthodox ways to identify areas to improve

Is a proponent of continuous improvement and innovation

Is never satisfied with the status quo

Understands the criticality of innovation

Balances demand for innovation with costs associated

Knows when innovation or improvements are not really necessary

### Negative Phrases

Is unable to come up with new approaches

Needs to work outside the box

Avoids new methods

Lacks a creative mind-set

Tries to use the same solution to every problem

Is unable to come up with cost-saving ideas

Tries to reinvent the wheel

Comes up with highly impractical solutions

Thinks up solutions that are rarely feasible

Solutions create more problems than they solve

# Interpersonal Skills

These are people skills. They involve using all modes of communication (oral, written, nonverbal) to motivate, convince, and gain assistance and support from others, in order to achieve your goals.

## Positive Phrases

Is very adept in situations of conflict

Is a strong communicator

Chooses the right words

Knows when to back off

Understands how to work with other cultures

Is a soft-spoken leader who uses his interpersonal skills well

Is effective with people in stressful situations

Has the ability to calm others in the face of a crisis

Is an excellent listener who is highly regarded for his feedback

Is very persuasive when necessary

Never speaks a bad or derogatory word

## Interpersonal Skills *continued*

Is sensitive to employees' needs

Is an excellent reader of body language

Is highly respected by peers for his or her straight-forwardness

Pursues outside courses to continually improve performance

Strives to be current with technology

Is a superb negotiator

### Negative Phrases

Has bad table manners

Turns others off

Is poorly thought of

Creates tension when dealing with others

Has very little tact

Needs to think before speaking

Does not listen to others

Refuses to make concessions when negotiating

Needs to gain empathy for others

Increases hostility through lack of understanding

Uses body language that puts others off

Uses inappropriate gestures

Does not understand cultural protocol

Talks down to others

Is demeaning to others

Makes inappropriate comments

Makes inappropriate jokes

Says things that are culturally insensitive

# Job Knowledge

Along with general job knowledge, every employee needs knowledge specific to his or her position. Employees need to possess necessary knowledge about what's to be done, how, and why and understand the facts, skills, processes, inputs, and outputs of their job.

## Positive Phrases

Possesses total understanding of job and role in company

Continually acquires new knowledge

Seeks to know everything related to position

Is well rounded in all areas of know-how

Knows the basics of job

Is very knowledgeable in processes associated with work

Has in-depth knowledge of job functions

## Job Knowledge *continued*

Is always reading up on new techniques

Learns new work content quickly

Brings significant know-how to position

Successfully applies relevant knowledge to job

### Negative Phrases

Is not fully knowledgeable about job

Has difficulty grasping entire job

Needs refresher course in process management

Claims to know all there is to know about the job

Is unprepared for his or her job

Needs a review of job basics before doing more work

Has difficulty applying what he or she knows

Is not totally up to speed with job foundations

Needs additional course work

Would benefit from job coaching

Lacks necessary understanding of fundamentals

# Judgment

Judgment is the ability to correctly arrive at conclusions or opinions about people, things, actions, decisions, etc. Good judgment comes from experience, sound analysis, and sometimes calculated hunches.

## Positive Phrases

Exercises sound judgment

Is objective in assessments of fellow employees

Does not rush to judgment but seeks inputs before deciding

Can successfully assess situation with limited data

Is highly respected for opinions and decisions

Arrives at decisions in an orderly fashion

Is good at making judgments with limited information

Seeks inputs and opinions from others before passing judgment

Has a core set of values upon which decisions are made

Informs others of his or her intentions before broadcasting decision

Acknowledges when a bad choice is made

Makes judgments with company and employees in mind

## Judgment *continued*

Is open to changing earlier decision if new facts surface

Is very objective in his or her judgment of others

Does not allow hearsay to affect his or her judgment

Keeps cost considerations in mind when making decisions

Relies on facts and probabilities when passing judgment

Is not quick to judge others

### Negative Phrases

Rushes to judgment without all the necessary information

Is highly judgmental of others

Is reluctant to make even the simplest of decisions

Lacks experience to make important decisions

Does not seek inputs of others when deciding on action

Judgment is sometimes flawed

Takes big chances

Leaves out important considerations when making choices

Is overly subjective in the judgment process

Is not a good judge of people's ability

Is too critical of people

Won't form own opinions

Often changes mind

# Leadership

The capacity or ability to lead people, and to provide direction and guidance to others, is an important skill at all levels of employment, CEO and mailroom clerk alike.

## Positive Phrases

Builds strong teams

Plans employees' work

Possesses good organization skills

Has staff respect and they follow his or her direction

Has vision and can explain it to employees

Sets goals and identifies actions

Instills commitment on behalf of team members

Has strong sense of right and wrong

Is consistent with personal values

Mobilizes department in times of crisis

Delegates work among employees

## Leadership *continued*

Clarifies expectations and responds to concerns

Involves staff in decision-making process

Empowers people to do their jobs

Is tactful in difficult situations

Has strong budgeting know-how

Is impartial in dealings with staff and peers

Maintains good balance between company goals and employee needs

Pays for performance

Creates a positive environment and makes it motivating

Is powerful in persuasion

Helps employees overcome barriers to work achievement

Instills quality orientation with employees

Strives to learn and apply latest leadership tools

### Negative Phrases

Has a tendency to make decisions without involving personnel

Leads a team reluctant to follow direction

Does not have respect of department

Over-relies on power of position to lead team

Keeps employees in the dark as to decisions and expectations

Is not consistent with decisions

Is a poor judge of people

People are not 100 percent behind decisions and direction

Has a too-authoritarian leadership style

Doesn't understand capabilities of individual team members

Doesn't work at establishing relationships with staff

Has infrequent interaction with staff

Communicates via e-mail rather than in person

## Motivation

Motivation is the desire and drive to achieve, get work done, and make a difference. In combination with job knowledge and experience, motivation is what makes one successful.

The highly motivated person can move mountains for you even if he or she is limited in job knowledge and experience. Know what and how to motivate your employees, and you will see new results.

## Motivation *continued*

### Positive Phrases

Is highly self-motivated

Tackles even the most distasteful of tasks

Has a high level of drive

Is very motivated to succeed

Is tenacious

Never gives up

Responds to suggestions

Has pure motives when taking on work

Takes little to get motivated to take on more

Is motivated by desire to help others

Always sees the benefit of doing things right

Requires no supervision; is motivated to do the job

Likes to accomplish goals

Always goes the extra mile

Wants to make a difference in job

Continually seeks achievement

### Negative Phrases

Is not excited about work

Avoids difficult tasks

Does only the bare minimum

Is not interested in being the best

Is not internally driven

Takes a lot of prodding to get the job done

Must be coaxed to take on extra work

Never does things on his or her own

Gives up easily

Does not follow through

Prefers to do just enough to get by

Won't take the necessary time to do the job right

# Multitasking

Multitasking is the ability to perform two or more simultaneous tasks. It's a delicate balancing act and requires the employee to prioritize, organize, coordinate, and perform several subtasks within each task without any loss in quality for any project.

## Positive Phrases

Can perform a number of tasks simultaneously

Is excellent at multitasking

Meets all deadlines for several ongoing projects

Manages several concurrent tasks effectively

Delegates nonessential tasks to vendors

## Multitasking *continued*

Can handle multiple projects

Balances needs and resources to complete tasks on time

Performs many tasks at once without reducing quality

Maintains focus when dealing with several tasks

Can handle a large workload

Completes low-priority tasks during downtime

Balances several simultaneous projects well

### Negative Phrases

Can only do one thing at a time

Performs poorly when working on more than one project

Is unable to multitask

Loses focus when working on several simultaneous projects

Does not complete all concurrent projects

Misses details when more than one task is being processed

Cannot handle a large and varied workload

Prioritizes and completes simultaneous tasks poorly

# Chapter 7

# General Phrases by Attribute: O–P

Even the best system can have its pitfalls. It's essential that you realize the implications of what you're evaluating. Some systems reward "safe" approaches, even for innovators or problem-solvers who need to take risks to be successful. Others motivate employees to "beat the system." Whatever your system is and whatever you measure, be sure to constantly ask yourself, "Am I measuring the right things? What values will this process instill? Will it motivate or unmotivate?"

# Organization

Organization involves forethought. It's the process of knowing what resources are needed and systematizing and managing them. An organized system is efficient, streamlined, and easier to use for all involved.

## Positive Phrases

Realistic about capabilities

Generates meaningful work plans

Is well organized with support material

Anticipates obstacles to plans

Is systematic in approach to work

Produces detailed documentation

Involves others in planning process

Is always prepared

Sets up systems

Is timely with follow-up

Manages multiple projects efficiently

Identifies resources needed to accomplish plan

Sets achievable schedules

## Negative Phrases

Is overly optimistic with projections

Underestimates time required to complete task

Is routinely surprised

Is often unprepared

Takes on more than he or she can handle

Has a disorganized approach

Needs to develop a system

Would benefit from a more systematic approach

Produces sloppy work

Lets things slip through

Misses deadlines

Forgets important details

Fails to develop a plan of attack

Does everything by feel

Has difficulty finding things

Forgets location of documents

# Personal Attributes

Personal attributes relate to the individual's physical, mental, and emotional characteristics. This only includes attributes that are directly related to job performance.

## Personal Attributes *continued*

### Positive Phrases

Is able to safely lift 25 pounds as required for the position

Shows excellent interpersonal skills

Is well liked and well thought of

Has a high regard for others

Places company needs before his or her own needs

Is easy to work with

Gets along well with others

Takes constructive criticism well

Knows how to take charge when appropriate

Is a quick learner

Follows directions

Has proven to be honorable

Keeps promises

Maintains relationships with customers

Pitches in where needed

Follows manager's suggestions

Is honest

Has a corporate appearance

Proceeds in a professional manner

## Negative Phrases

Has been caught lying

Has a sloppy appearance

Does not live up to promises made

Is frequently not properly groomed

Others have complained about his or her hygiene

Wears ill-fitting or inappropriate attire

Has an arrogant manner

Is difficult to get along with

Has problems dealing with others

Is defensive when suggestions are made

Is slow to learn new things

Gives up easily

Brags to others

Procrastinates

Does not take direction well

Does not follow directions

Is easily distracted

Takes things personally

Is quick to show off

# Persuasiveness

Persuasiveness is the ability to demonstrate ideas and convince others of their validity. You might think this is only applicable in sales or marketing positions, but every employee needs strong powers of persuasion from time to time.

## Positive Phrases

Gains understanding through discussion

Gets others to agree

Finds common ground

Breaks deadlocked situations

Gains respect from others

Presents ideas well

Is sensitive to others' goals

Is committed to mutual satisfaction

Explains clearly

Makes strong supporting points

Uses visual aids to increase understanding

Is empathetic

Understands the needs of others

Presents information from others' point of view

Understands the factors that motivate

Gathers information before presenting

Understands what works for different audiences

Customizes presentations toward listeners' experience

Knows when to push back and when to concede

Uses excellent rebuttals

Mitigates objections

## Negative Phrases

Makes weak cases

Presents ideas in an incomprehensive manner

Does not explain thoroughly

Only sees things from his or her point of view

Does not understand motivating factors of others

Tries to convince people who don't have decision-making authority

Talks incessantly

Does not ask questions of those he or she is trying to persuade

Is unable to elicit desired responses from presentations

Has a cutthroat mentality

Is overly aggressive

Does not have credibility

Rarely has all the facts prior to discussion

Does not plan for objections

## Persuasiveness *continued*

Fails to learn about client prior to consultation

Does not present information in a flowing manner

## Planning

Planning is the ability to use knowledge and past experience, along with a review of resources, to decide how best to tackle a set of issues. Parts of the planning process are usually prioritization, situational awareness, research, and a proposed course of action.

### Positive Phrases

Plans things well in advance

Does not procrastinate

Finishes assignments in plenty of time for changes

Anticipates problems before they arise

Develops sensible plans

Delivers projects on time

Is consistently within budget

Puts plans into action

Assesses resources needed to bring plans into action

Balances plans with company needs

Develops contingency plans

Identifies potential problems

Plans for unexpected issues

Lets manager know a project's limitations

Lets manager know his or her own limitations

Has a strategic vision for each project

Uses checklists for action plans to ensure completion

Has long-, medium-, and short-range plans and goals

Establishes goals and objectives prior to creating a plan

## Negative Phrases

Plans everything last minute

Does not plan at all

Fails to utilize a plan

Does not follow the plan

Rarely plans for problems

Creates unrealistic plans

Produces plans that have large gaps

Does not research needs prior to planning

Offers no alternatives in plans

# Potential for Advancement

Potential for advancement is seen in those individuals who continually are able to take on new and more advanced responsibilities.

Reviewing potential for advancement is one area that will be highly customized based on the position. An engineer who is promoted to a senior engineer position needs vastly different skills from those a salesperson promoted to a sales manager needs. In addition to the following suggestions, you can create other phrases by using the job description from the position to which the individual may be promoted.

## Positive Phrases

Shows great potential

Is ready to handle additional responsibilities

Has a deep knowledge of the entire process

Is insightful into numbers and processes

Sees the company as a whole

Has an overall view

Shows great leadership ability

Can motivate others

Is looked up to by peers

Coaches effectively

Helps others improve

Is ready for the next step

Is ready for leadership training

Has a bright future in this company

## Negative Phrases

Has stopped learning months ago

Avoids new responsibilities

Demonstrates no leadership skills

Has a microscopic view

Is adverse to taking risk

Enjoys the status quo

Does not want more responsibility

Is unwilling to help peers

Needs to learn to train others

Is not emotionally disciplined

Wavers on decisions

Shows uncertainty in front of others

# Prioritizing

Prioritizing is the ability to determine the urgency and importance of several tasks and decide in which order to perform them. Some managers assign priority to employees' projects. Other employees need to assess the work they have and set their own priorities.

## Prioritizing *continued*

### Positive Phrases

Knows what needs to be done first

Establishes priorities

Handles most urgent matters first

Does not get sidetracked by minor issues

Sees the big picture

Avoids distractions

Focuses on the goals at hand

Handles lower-priority projects when appropriate

Identifies projects that add little or no value

Sets aside time for planning and prioritizing

Is excellent at time management

Is able to make priority decisions

Uses time and energy efficiently

Eliminates all nonessential functions

### Negative Phrases

Fails to prioritize

Gets jobs done in no particular order

Spends too much time on minor tasks

Does not spend the appropriate amount of time on critical projects

Handles tasks that add little or no value

Wastes time on side projects

Misses important deadlines due to getting side-tracked

Does not handle important jobs in a timely manner

Needs to learn to properly prioritize

Has priorities not aligned with company needs

# Problem-Solving

Problem-solving is usually a three-part process. First, a problem must be diagnosed so that the actual problem is clear (there may be more than one). Additionally, the perceived problem may either have deeper roots or may be unrelated to the symptom. Then it must be researched so decisions can be made.

## Positive Phrases

Finds simple solutions to tough problems

Diagnoses and fixes problems

Finds several solutions and determines the best approach

Is an excellent troubleshooter

Prevents problems from occurring in the future

## Problem-Solving *continued*

Gets to the root of the issue

Understands the entire problem before trying to fixing it

Tests to ensure problem is eliminated

Tries several solutions to find the best one

Determines when repair is appropriate

Verifies whether a problem is worth fixing

Ensures repair will not cause new problems

Has resources to make necessary changes when problems arise

### Negative Phrases

Fails to accurately diagnose problems

Is unable to find solutions when problems arise

Just patches visible problems without getting to the underlying cause

Does not look into other manifestations of the problem

Uses the same solution to every problem

Poorly patches problems, which leads to bigger problems

Comes up with solutions that cause other problems

Offers few suggestions when problems occur

Does not research issues before recommending action

Does not have the knowledge to solve problems

Needs to gain better troubleshooting skills

# Productivity

Productivity refers to the amount of relevant and useful work an individual can generate. The key to productivity is that an employee generates *useful* work. Someone can be very busy and get a lot done; if the work isn't useful and relevant, however, it isn't productive. Be sure to carefully define, measure, and express the actions and outcome you expect of an employee, or you may find that a lot of effort is wasted.

## Positive Phrases

Has increased production by *X* percent

Maintains target manufacturing ratio

Has lower defects rate than peers

Consistently finds ways to increase production

Always exceeds demand

Streamlines processes

Decreases cost of goods sold

Reduces reject ratios

## **Productivity** *continued*

Increases throughput

Cuts time to produce

Decreases overtime

Trims headcount

Reduces equipment downtime

Increases safety statistics

Reduces delivery time

Lowers material costs

Optimizes tooling changeover time

Creates a just-in-time model

Exceeds production schedule

Delivers ahead of time

Mechanizes functions

Increases workflow

Codifies procedures

Defines problem areas and looks for solutions

Eliminates the weak links

Continually upgrades systems

Stays on the cutting edge

Holds self to a higher standard

Learns labor-saving methods

## Negative Phrases

Works on projects that have little value

Focuses on irrelevant factors

Is not in touch with technology

Produces less than peers by $X$ percent

Fails to meet production schedule

Increases delivery time

Adds personnel with no noticeable results

Delivers $X$ percent less than goal

Is unable to meet delivery schedule

Increases employee turnover

Does not upgrade machinery

Refuses to replace underperforming _____

Spends too much time thinking and not enough time doing

Does not maintain machinery for peak performance

# Professional Development

Professional development encompasses the outside knowledge an employee has gained in his or her field. This can be technical knowledge, new credentials earned, or a new depth of understanding.

# Professional Development
## *continued*

## Positive Phrases

Continually learns and grows

Is objective about capabilities and wants to expand

Seeks advice

Sets high standards for learning

Isn't afraid of taking on new challenges

Is open-minded to new methods

Embraces change

Is a quick learner

Is open to suggestions of others

Understands shortcomings

Shares needs with others and learns from their experience

Learns from top performers

Studies on his or her own time

Takes night courses

Reads industry and professional periodicals

Keeps current with trends and information

Participates in symposiums and workshops

Seeks expert advice

Invests in self

Finds new resources

## Negative Phrases

Has stopped growing in this position

Needs to start learning new skills

Has not maintained his or her credentials

Does not read industry materials

Did not attend offered training seminars

Is resistant to change

Maintains the status quo

Does not see the benefit of additional training

Relies on outdated methods

Believes he or she has all the answers

Avoids new challenges

Shuns new methods

Thinks there's nothing more to learn

Finds excuses not to improve

# Professionalism

Professionalism is the practice of proceeding in a businesslike, proficient, expedient, and ethical manner. This can apply to how a person dresses, speaks, carries him- or herself, and interacts with co-workers.

## Positive Phrases

Is well spoken

Dresses appropriately for work circumstances

Is highly respected

Is knowledgeable of job and profession/industry

Seeks and maintains professional credentials

Has built and earned an excellent reputation

Is viewed as a trusted adviser

Behaves in a businesslike and professional manner

Understands his or her responsibilities

Speaks with authority

Communicates with confidence

Treats others with respect

Is upstanding in his or her community

Behaves in an ethical manner

Maintains a neat, orderly appearance

## Negative Phrases

Talks down to others

Dresses inappropriately

Creates sloppy work

Is not well informed

Has a bad reputation

Is irresponsible with company resources

Has been dishonest with customers

Sacrifices quality for speed

Speaks in colloquialisms

Expresses inappropriate opinions

Uses foul language in the office

Uses sexual innuendo

Has been caught lying to his or her manager

Uses company resources for personal use

Engages in office politics

Gossips and talks negatively about others

Chapter **8**

# General Phrases by Attribute: Q–Z

As we continue listing sample phrases to help you describe employee performance on appraisal forms, keep in mind that the intent of these sample phrases is to spark thoughts about the most appropriate manner in which to describe one's work and behaviors. Take the samples, exchange words and adjectives, and throw in your own to make it reflect reality.

# Quality

In its simplest definition, quality means meeting expectations, doing things right, producing something to specifications. As a manager, one of your goals should be to produce quality employees as well as product.

## Positive Phrases

Follows company quality procedures

Uses work improvement process to reduce errors

Sets high-quality standards

Uses problem-solving techniques to overcome quality barriers

Is creative in reducing waste

Seldom makes mistakes

Continually thinks of ways to improve work and company results

Seeks continuous improvement

Learns and applies new methods and systems

Understands the importance of quality

Doesn't hide errors

Knows how to set and measure meaningful quality standards

Isn't satisfied with the status quo

Strives to improve personal abilities and standards

Offers suggestions for improvement

Utilizes benchmarking techniques

## Negative Phrases

Is not interested in doing quality work

Frequently cuts corners with work

Resists learning new quality-improvement techniques

Would benefit from a course on process control

Is more interested in quantity than quality

Doesn't pay full attention to work, thus causing errors

Fails to understand the importance of quality in work

Does not agree with company quality standards

Needs to think more about ways to improve quality

Lets teammates down by failing to share critical information on a timely basis

# Relationship-Building

Relationship-building is the art of building lasting, trustworthy business relationships with peers, colleagues, subordinates, bosses, clients, outsiders, suppliers, etc.

## **Relationship-Building** *continued*

### **Positive Phrases**

Is constantly working on maintaining internal relationships

Creates rapport immediately with new contacts

Goes the extra mile in cementing ongoing relationships

Has an extensive external network

Is always looking at ways to help others

Is very trustworthy with relationships

Can always be relied on by others in the office

Makes contacts effortlessly

Keeps confidential information confidential

Understands that relationships must be dynamic not one-time

Offers help and information to others even when not asked

Works his or her relationships in a low-key manner

Likes challenge of developing relationships with new people

Is very successful at job because of strong relationships

Does not take advantage of contacts, networks, or relationships

## Negative Phrases

Does not work at maintaining important relationships

Takes advantage of internal relationships

Is not always trusted by peers when handling confidential matters

Doesn't get out of office enough to work on external relationships

Is reluctant to network at association meetings

Does not see value in creating peer relationships

Is all business with staff; needs to build better relationships

Tests relationships by always asking but not giving

Can improve relationships by being more professional

Has a tendency to burn out by trying to do to much for others

## Resourcefulness

Resourceful individuals have the internal know-how and external resources to deal effectively with a new or unexpected situation. They are creative in overcoming barriers that may be in the way of securing information, support, etc.; they exhibit inventiveness.

## **Resourcefulness** *continued*

### **Positive Phrases**

Finds unusual solutions

Is able to improvise solutions

Does more with available resources than others

Finds new resources

Is able to custom build solutions with available materials

Quickly comes up with alternative methods to fix problems

Finds innovative solutions to real-time problems

Finds unorthodox resources to deal with issues

Is highly resourceful in many areas

Learns from past experiences

Is very creative in finding solutions to unexpected problems

Has a wealth of ideas when faced with new circumstances

Isn't afraid of trying new approaches

Responds quickly and knowledgeably to crises

Puts a new spin on things

Uses vast knowledge to innovate

Looks at problems in unusual ways to find uncommon solutions

## Negative Phrases

Lacks creativity when faced with new and unique challenges

Is afraid to go outside the box when tackling new situations

Prefers to use existing resources when dealing with new problems

Does not use network and relationships when short on ideas

Is afraid to take risks

Is great on ideas but short on delivery

Cannot see the big picture

Never sees a situation from the eyes of others

Doesn't want to admit failure

Tends to give up if first response doesn't work

## Supervision

Supervision deals with the skills and ability to direct or oversee the work of others, including training and coaching. Good supervisors plan and review the work of their subordinates and know their strengths, capabilities, and areas to watch.

## Supervision *continued*

### Positive Phrases

Clearly specifies requirements to subordinates

Excellent at recruiting and hiring department employees

Motivates team

Makes expectations clear

Measures results

Manages for results

Increased department productivity by *(state data)*

Works with below-standard employees to improve

Promotes from within when possible

Rewards positive behaviors

Gives excellent feedback

Provides continuous training

Establishes benchmarks for success

Takes responsibility for team's successes and failures

Specifies goals and follows through

Works with entire team to improve performance

Makes new resources available to team

Understands problems and helps others find solutions

Creates excitement and a sense of achievement when team hits goal

Redeploys good employees who are unable to perform at this job

Catches team's mistakes early

Is always accessible to department employees

Provides accurate and helpful appraisals

## Negative Phrases

Does not give clear work instructions

Sets low expectations of employees

Is very rigid in treatment of employees

Avoids tough tasks such as discipline

Doesn't get out on the floor enough; is desk-bound

Is not sensitive to employees' needs

Is not always equal in treatment of employee issues

Is not inclined to give workers timely feedback

Needs to develop better training plans for employees

Spends too much time coaching employees not qualified for work

Can't be reached when away from work site

Prefers to do work on own rather than train employees

Employees would like more frequent feedback

# Teamwork

Teamwork is the collaborative and collective effort of a group of employees to accomplish a defined, common goal. When your team is working together to achieve an end result, you're bound to be more successful.

## Positive Phrases

Works well with others

Handles team projects properly

Gets along with peers

Works by consensus

Agrees to timelines and follows through

Accepts leadership

Allows others to lead when appropriate

Leads by example

Picks up slack when not done by fellow teammates

Helps team find common ground

Keeps the goals of the project in mind

Delegates effectively

Volunteers to take on tasks

Does more than his or her share

Does not take things personally

Is able to lead or follow, depending on project needs

## Negative Phrases

Resists being part of a team; would rather work alone

Looks out only for self when on a team

Does not offer help to other team members

Does not carry own load when on a team

Is not suited for team projects

Needs to work on relationship building with teammates

Has a tendency to dominate team meetings

Often blames others when his or her own work is not done

Has a "What's in it for me?" attitude

Must be more focused on the value of teamwork

# Technical Abilities

Along with general and specific job knowledge, workers in some industries also need technical abilities, or the know-how and experience with technical matters such as processes, engineering, computers, science, etc.

## Technical Abilities *continued*

### Positive Phrases

Has a vast knowledge of systems

Understands process intuitively

Produces fine-quality work

Knows the most modern methods

Reads relevant trade journals

Continually learns about new technical arenas

Is very knowledgeable in this area

Has a high degree of expertise

Is an industry expert

Can create tactical plans

Has new ideas about solving existing technical issues

Recently completed *(training or school)* program

Maintains professional credentials

Sees value in continuing education

Is one of the best in the field

### Negative Phrases

Has tendency to rely on old technical knowledge

Is reluctant to take evening classes

Is amazingly bright but will not share knowledge with others

Is not certified

Does not see need to complete a B.S. degree

Is very knowledgeable but rushes work and makes errors

Needs to attend more symposiums in his or her field

Can't advance if uninterested in pursuing advanced degree

Has difficulty expressing self when dealing with technical data

# Thoroughness

Work or action is very complete, accurate, comprehensive, or exact. Employee's work is not missing anything. He or she looks at all possibilities and scenarios, and leaves nothing to chance.

## Positive Phrases

Always thorough in investigation of process errors

Strives to cover all possibilities

Work content is beyond expectations and very exacting

Is never satisfied until all options are explored

Never relies on subjective data

## Thoroughness *continued*

Finishes every last detail of each project

Triple-checks all work

Wants work to be very accurate

Is demanding of self and work detail

Works meticulously

## Negative Phrases

Overlooks small but important details

Needs to be more thorough with problem analysis

Not inclined to go the extra distance when proofing work

Needs to be more diligent and exacting with research protocols

Tends to just scratch the surface with work content

Relies too much on intuition rather than fact

Not suited for projects where in-depth analysis is required

Often turns in incomplete work

Ignores large portions of assignments

Work lacks required polished look and feel

# Time Management

In today's fast-paced world, time management is key. How well an employee masters his or her use of time, setting priorities, dealing with paperwork, interruptions and telephone calls, attending meetings, meeting deadlines, etc., can make all the difference.

Because there's a finite amount of time in everyone's day and productivity is essential, time management becomes one of the most essential factors for employees to work on. This includes working efficiently during peak time and using time wisely during downtime. Side projects, low-priority jobs, and preparation for peak time are superb uses of downtime.

## Positive Phrases

Is very effective in use and allocation of time

Is highly organized in work

Makes excellent use of PDA

Allows ample time to complete projects and work

Effectively schedules each day's activities

Prioritizes work and immediately addresses most important items

Bundles phone calls and does at the end of the day

## Time Management *continued*

Has learned to block out time without interruptions for key work

Lets staff know his or her schedule

Utilizes a daily planner to optimize his or her schedule

Has an extensive to-do list

Minimizes time in meetings

Gets work done during day so it doesn't have to be taken home

Has taken a time-management course and has applied what he or she learned there

Keeps conversations to a minimum; gets right to the point

Never misses a deadline

### Negative Phrases

Has a tendency to ramble and waste time

Has an unorganized calendar

Has too many interruptions; needs to block out solo time

Answers telephone rather than having assistant screen calls

Is often inaccessible to staff

Is always in meetings; needs to delegate

Avoids doing the tough tasks

Is a procrastinator with unpleasant tasks

Is frequently late with work

Misses deadlines

Always asks for more time to complete work

Does not do effective job of planning and scheduling work

# Timeliness

Being appropriate or opportune in timing of one's actions. He or she completes work or projects in a timely manner, and results are on schedule.

## Positive Phrases

Arrives to meetings on time

Takes breaks at appropriate times

Returns from breaks in a timely fashion

Returns from meetings at scheduled times

Is always punctual with reports

Has an excellent sense of timing with publications

Has a strong sense of knowing when to speak up

Brings perspective to the situation just when it's needed

Times new product releases just right

## Timeliness *continued*

Understands people and when to introduce change

Manages multiple projects simultaneously

Is right on time with engineering modifications

Is proactive and thus allows for timely resolution of problems

### Negative Phrases

Frequently shows up late for work

Takes longer than scheduled breaks

Leaves work early

Procrastination creates lateness in product forecasts

Tends to have poor timing with sales-incentive rollouts

Does not understand the time parameters involved with projects

Is always late with critical employee training

Has great ideas but no grasp of deployment time

Criticisms of staff are often premature

# Trainability

The degree to which someone can learn new things, information, work procedures, skills, knowledge, work techniques, etc. The ability or knack of grasping and applying new knowledge, behaviors, tools, and processes. Trainability doesn't have to do with one's willingness to learn but rather one's mental capacity or background to learn new things.

## Positive Phrases

Likes to learn

Appreciates guidance

Understands new ideas quickly

Studies on his or her own

Practices and reviews new material

Takes constructive criticism well

Is open to suggestions

Is willing to try new methods

Is able to take risks

Learns from others

Follows examples

Watches others for new ideas

Follows directions

Is responsive to coaching

## Trainability *continued*

### Negative Phrases

Resists new ideas

Wants to do things his or her own way

Refuses to study materials

Becomes defensive when suggestions are made

Has to learn everything for himself or herself

Does not believe he or she can learn the material

Does not try to learn new information

Is afraid to learn

Fears new ideas

Does not value the material

Is resistant to coaching

Does not have the capacity to learn new processes.

Requires additional training time to grasp work methods

Despite having learned new techniques, refuses to put them to use

Does not retain, over time, new procedures for processing

# Pop Performance Phrases

You may be restricted to using the "lingo" of your company's performance appraisal process and forms, or you may have some latitude in using your own descriptors. Either way, in the end, it can sometimes feel like you're assigning Superman ratings:

1. Leaps over two-story buildings
2. Leaps over hi-rise buildings
3. Leaps over skyscrapers
4. Can't leap at all

The system your company uses or the one you create should be a simple spectrum of statements. Here are some typical groupings and phrases:

Exceeds all expectations

Exceeds most expectations

Meets all expectations and exceeds some

Meets all expectations

Meets most but not all expectations

Meets some expectations

Does not meet expectations

Outstanding

Excellent

Very good

Above average

Good/average

Below average

Unacceptable

Superior

Acceptable

Fair

Substandard

 **Performance Pointers**

When you make a statement about an employee's performance, you must be able to substantiate it with examples of the person's work. Often the rating is done in a comparative (and competitive) environment, and the ratings can be relative to others in the same department. Some organizations set concrete examples of performance levels with correlating descriptors.

These "pop phrases" are also useful for evaluations in which human resources provides a list of attributes and the manager is left to fill in the blanks.

Similarly, if your company uses a number ranking system, try to think of the numbers in terms of the phrases provided in this chapter's list. For example, you could assign 6 to "Outstanding," 5 to "Excellent," and so on, and fill out the appraisal that way.

One difficulty in rating people is that employees equate ratings of "Acceptable," "Average," and "Good" with their school days and equate such reviews with a C grade. To get around this, try using "Meets expectations."

# 3
## What to Say: Words

In the past chapters, we've given you many examples of phrases that accurately assess performance. This list is by no means exhaustive. Following our model, you can create your own phrases for particular functions specific to your company, department, or individual job. In Part 3, we give you lists of verbs, adverbs, and adjectives you can use to formulate your own phrases. Each phrase should have a minimum of two parts: it should contain the item you want to assess (i.e., computer skills) and also a verb, adverb, or adjective that describes how the function was performed. You can also use the words in the following chapters to modify a phrase in the preceding chapters so it more accurately describes your employee's performance.

# Adverbs That Accurately Assess Performance

A basic phrase can be turned into a strong, exact statement of an employee's performance by adding an appropriate adverb. Adverbs modify verbs; therefore, if you want to qualify or expand the meaning of the verb, add an adverb. The selection of adverbs from which you can choose is endless.

Because adverbs add strength to your choice of verbs, remember to be accurate and objective with their use. You are not evaluating the employee as a person; rather, you are evaluating the person's performance. This should be based on facts, never on personal feelings.

Here are some examples of correct use of verbs, adjectives, and adverbs:

- Bill frequently shows up to work 30 minutes late.

- Jennifer never has missed work unexpectedly.

And here are some examples of incorrect use of verbs, adjectives, and adverbs:

- Fred is wasteful.
- Caron is lazy.

**DANGER** **Performance Pitfalls** _____

> Adverbs are more difficult to use for an appraisal because they imply a value judgment that may seem arbitrary. To avoid this, be sure you back up your statement with solid examples. An employee's incident file can be a useful source to find these examples.

Here are some adverbs to help you accurately describe an employee's performance:

Angrily

Awkwardly

Badly

Beautifully

Better

Blindly

Briefly

Carefully

Carelessly

Cautiously

Cheerfully

Clumsily

Defiantly

Easily

Elegantly

Enthusiastically

Exactly

Happily

Horribly

Hungrily

Magnificently

Mortally

Optimistically

Ordinarily

Pessimistically

Politely

Poorly

Powerfully

Promptly

Punctually

Quickly

Quietly

Rarely

Recklessly

Regularly

Reluctantly

Repeatedly

Rudely

Safely

Seriously

Silently

Stealthily

Stingily

Successfully

Suddenly

Suspiciously

Testily

Thoroughly

Thoughtfully

Truthfully

Unexpectedly

Wastefully

Wonderfully

# Adjectives That Accurately Assess Performance

Adjectives turn a dull noun into something that shines or sears. Nouns, when used alone, may not totally describe what you're saying about a person's performance. Add an adjective and, voilà!, the noun now takes on gradations. Adjectives add to the intent of the feedback and help the employee truly understand how he or she is doing. As always, be prepared to back up your choice of adjective and noun with concrete, memorable performance situations.

Absent

Adaptable

Advanced

Adventurous

Aggressive

Ambitious

Bad

Better

Biased

Big

Bright

Careful

Clever

Clumsy

Committed

Credible

Decent

Dedicated

Dependant

Dull

Enthusiastic

Excited

Fair

Fine

Frail

Friendly

Funny

Gifted

Gigantic

Good

Great

Grumpy

Happy

Hardworking

Honest

Horrible

Independent

Kind

Long

Magnificent

Many

Mighty

Modest

Moral

New

Nice

Odd

Open-minded

Ordinary

Patient

Practical

Precious

Prickly

Quick

Quickest

Quiet

Radical

Rare

Relaxed

Robust

Secure

Serious

Sincere

Skillful

Stingy

Strange

Successful

Talented

Testy

Tenacious

Tough

Tricky

Unique

Vast

Wasteful

Well-informed

Wonderful

# Verbs That Describe Actions

Verbs are the essence of performance appraisal statements. The verb is the beginning of an action. Most job description statements begin with verbs as they describe the action or work to be taken or done. Depending on the work discipline, specific verbs are repeatedly used and well understood by the professional community.

The easiest approach to performance appraisal phrasings is to begin with the very same statement used in the job description and then quantify or qualify the statement with an adverb or adjective. For example, if the job description says, "prepares weekly production report," then a possible appraisal statement of results might be, "carefully prepares weekly production report and always ahead of the deadline."

# Adaptability

Adjusted

Assimilated

Augmented

Collaborated

Combined

Condensed

Diversified

Expanded

Formed

Improved

Launched

Liquidated

Localized

Modified

Proposed

Reconciled

Reduced

Remodeled

Revamped

Revised

Saved

# Clerical/Administrative

Approved

Arranged

Assisted

Carried out

Catalogued

Classified

Collected

Compiled

Consulted with

Contributed

Dispatched

Executed

Filed

Generated

Helped

Implemented

Inspected

Monitored

Notified

Observed

Operated

Organized

Performed

Prepared

Processed

Purchased

Recorded

Retrieved

Routed

Screened

Specified

Supported

Systematized

Tabulated

Validated

Verified

Volunteered

## Communication

Addressed

Arbitrated

Arranged

Authored

Briefed

Consulted

Corresponded

Demonstrated

Developed

Directed

Drafted

Edited

Enlisted

Exhibited

Explained

Formulated

Illustrated

Influenced

Interpreted

Lectured

Mediated

Moderated

Motivated

Negotiated

Persuaded

Presented

Promoted

Proved

Publicized

Published

Reconciled

Recorded

Reported

Researched

Settled

Solved

Spoke

Summarized

Translated

Wrote

## Creative

Acted

Conceived

Conceptualized

Created

Designed

Developed

Directed

Established

Expanded

Fashioned

Founded

Illustrated

Initiated

Instituted

Integrated

Introduced

Invented

Launched

Originated

Performed

Planned

Revitalized

Set up

Shaped

Visualized

## Efficiency

Accelerated

Advanced

Applied

Centralized

Cut

Doubled

Earned

Elevated

Eliminated

Enhanced

Enlarged

Expedited

Explored

Increased

Judged

Maintained

Minimized

Modernized

Optimized

Reinforced

Tripled

Vitalized

# Financial

Administered

Allocated

Analyzed

Appraised

Assessed

Audited

Balanced

Budgeted

Calculated

Compared

Computed

Defined

Detected

Developed

Estimated

Examined

Forecasted

Financed

Inspected

Invested

Investigated

Managed

Marketed

Observed

Originated

Pinpointed

Planned

Projected

Researched

Solved

Surveyed

Updated

## Leadership/Training

Adapted

Advised

Assessed

Clarified

Coached

Convinced

Communicated

Coordinated

Counseled

Critiqued

Developed

Educated

Enabled

Encouraged

Evaluated

Explained

Facilitated

Familiarized

Guided

Hired

Informed

Initiated

Instructed

Motivated

Persuaded

Prescribed

Promoted

Recruited

Referred

Regulated

Rehabilitated

Represented

Set goals

Settled

Staffed

Standardized

Stimulated

Terminated

## Management

Administered

Allocated

Analyzed

Assigned

Attained

Chaired

Conducted

Consolidated

Contracted

Coordinated

Delegated

Demonstrated

Developed

Directed

Engaged

Evaluated

Executed

Guided

Implemented

Improved

Increased

Led

Managed

Monitored

Organized

Oversaw

Planned

Prioritized

Produced

Recommended

Reviewed

Scheduled

Strengthened

Structured

Supervised

# Research

Clarified

Collected

Critiqued

Diagnosed

Evaluated

Examined

Extracted

Identified

Inspected

Interpreted

Interviewed

Invented

Investigated

Organized

Reviewed

Summarized

Surveyed

Systematized

## Technical

Assembled

Built

Calculated

Cleaned

Coded

Compiled

Computed

Constructed

Debugged

Designed

Devised

Diagnosed

Engineered

Fabricated

Gathered

Installed

Kept

Maintained

Operated

Overhauled

Prepared

Programmed

Ran

Refined

Remodeled

Repaired

Selected

Solved

Synthesized

Trained

Upgraded